F

LUCENT LIBRARY *of* HISTORICAL ERAS

Daily Life in Colonial America

DON NARDO

LUCENT BOOKS
A part of Gale, Cengage Learning

GALE
CENGAGE Learning™

Detroit • New York • San Francisco • New Haven, Conn • Waterville, Maine • London

LIBRARY OF CONGRESS CATALOGING-IN-PUBLICATION DATA

Nardo, Don, 1947-
  Daily life in colonial America / by Don Nardo.
    p. cm. -- (Lucent library of historical eras)
  Includes bibliographical references and index.
   ISBN 978-1-4205-0264-0 (hardcover)
   1. United States--Social life and customs--To 1775--Juvenile literature.
   2. United States--History--Colonial period, ca. 1600-1775--Juvenile literature. I. Title.
   E162.N37 2010
   973.2--dc22

                                                              2009045636

Lucent Books
27500 Drake Rd.
Farmington Hills, MI 48331

ISBN-13: 978-1-4205-0264-0
ISBN-10: 1-4205-0264-6

Printed in the United States of America
   3 4 5 6 7 14 13 12 11

Printed by Bang Printing, Brainerd, MN, 3rd Ptg., 08/2011

Contents

Foreword

Looking back from the vantage point of the present, history can be viewed as a myriad of intertwining roads paved by human events. Some paths stand out—broad highways whose mileposts, even from a distance of centuries, are clear. The events that propelled the rise to power of Germany's Third Reich, its role in World War II, and its eventual demise, for example, are well defined and documented.

Other roads are less distinct, their route sometimes hidden from view. Modern legislatures may have developed from old tribal councils, for example, but the links between them are indistinct in places, open to discussion and interpretation.

The architecture of civilization—law, religion, art, science, and government—as well as the more everyday aspects of our culture—what we eat, what we wear—all developed along the historical roads and byways. In that progression can be traced every facet of modern life.

A broad look back along these roads reveals that many paths—though of vastly different character—seem to converge at a few critical junctions. These intersections are those great historical eras that echo over the long, steady course of human history, extending beyond the past and into the present.

These epic periods of time are the focus of Historical Eras. They shine through the mists of history like beacons, illuminated by a burst of creativity that propels events forward—so bright that we, from thousands of years away, can clearly see the chain of events leading to the present.

Each Historical Eras consists of a set of books that highlight various aspects of these major eras. For example, the Elizabethan England library features volumes on Queen Elizabeth I and her court, Elizabethan theater, the great playwrights, and everyday life in Elizabethan London.

The mini-library approach allows for the division of each era into its most significant and most interesting parts and the exploration of those parts in depth. Also, social and cultural trends as well as illustrative documents and eyewitness accounts can be prominently featured in individual volumes.

Historical Eras presents a wealth of information to young readers. The lively narrative, fully documented primary and secondary source quotations, maps, photographs, sidebars, and annotated bibliographies serve as launching points for class discussion and further research.

In studying the great historical eras, students also develop a better understanding of our own times. What we learn from the past and how we apply it in the present may shape the future and may determine whether our era will be a guiding light to those traveling future roads.

ISLANDS IN THE WILDERNESS

Today most Americans live in cities and towns. Roughly 84 percent of the population dwells in communities of forty-five to fifty thousand people or more. And the rest, about 16 percent, live in smaller towns and more isolated rural areas. This distribution of people has a direct bearing on everyday life in the United States. It means that a majority of Americans grow up in houses or apartments with neighbors within earshot, attend moderate-to-large-size schools, and shop in sprawling malls and huge supermarkets.

Life in England's thirteen North American colonies was just the opposite. Most people lived in rural areas, and for a long time there were no sizable cities. In fact, at first there was a rather stark contrast between lands inhabited by whites and seen as "civilized" and those inhabited by animals and Indi-

ans and seen as "uncivilized." When the first English and other European settlers arrived in the early 1600s, they viewed the continent as a vast stretch of wilderness. As historians James M. Volo and Dorothy D. Volo point out,

> most areas of the world considered wilderness today are remote, inhospitable, or bereft of natural resources. Regions filled with wildlife, timber, fresh water, and fertile soil, as was America in the seventeenth and eighteenth centuries, generally do not [qualify as] a wilderness [area].[1]

Yet many, if not most, of the early settlers agreed with one of the leaders of the Plymouth Colony, William Bradford. He described the land he entered when stepping off the *Mayflower* as "a hideous and desolate wilderness filled with evil and capable of making man revert to savagery."[2] The reasons for this attitude are uncertain, especially when contrasted with the attitude of the Native Americans who already inhabited the region. Volo and Volo note that

> in Europe, the mountain peaks and cliffsides were the only landforms that had not been put into production by the sixteenth century. Possibly [this is why] many Europeans tended to link the concept of wilderness with uncultivated land that was rocky, heavily wooded, and inhabited only by wild beasts and [Indians]. By comparison, native Americans [did not see it as] wilderness. Indian religions accepted a relationship between man and the natural regions [that] bordered on love. They recognized man as one with all living things. Moreover, for them the wilderness did not have connotations of evil and disorder, but rather those of natural order.[3]

Far More Isolated Lives

Whatever the settlers' reasons for viewing the land as wilderness, there is no doubt that their primary goal was to tame it. That first entailed clearing the land of vegetation so farms and towns could be built. In those days, farms were the chief centers of life and production. The town centers, which were tiny by modern standards, served mainly as centralized depots for maintaining commerce with the mother country and other colonies. Also, the town was where the church and the seat of government (at first a simple meetinghouse) rested; but in those days most of the people who attended the church and ran the government lived outside the town on farms.

Furthermore, as time went on the outlying farms became increasingly distant from the town center. In 1635, only five years after English settlers established Boston in the Massachusetts Bay Colony, a law passed requiring all residents to build their farmhouses no more than half a mile from the central meetinghouse. In 1640, however, that statute had to be repealed. The lure of what seemed to be free land drew the settlers farther and farther outward. As Lehmann College scholar David F. Hawke explains, they steadily moved "away from the village, beyond the sound of the church bell, into the wilderness." And "until they created hamlets that eventually became villages [of their own], they were denizens [residents] of the forest."[4]

During the decades when farmers were taming what they saw as wilderness, they lived far more isolated lives than did their relatives and friends who lived or worked on farms back in England. In the mother country the population density was a good deal higher. There, as Hawke says, a short walk brought a farmer "the companionship of the local pub or tavern. A host of craftsmen—sawyers, blacksmiths, coopers, carpenters, wheelwrights—lay near at hand when needed." For early American farmers,

In early colonial times, a central meetinghouse usually served as the town gathering spot for most areas. The majority of people lived on farms far outside of town.

however, "such close community ties all but vanished." An average farmer and his family "lived semi-secluded lives, the nearest neighbor often no closer than a half a mile or so."[5]

To establish their new lives in these isolated spots, the early settlers had to accomplish enormous amounts of back-breaking work. And they did so with only a few, mainly unsophisticated tools. According to Louis B. Wright, a noted expert on colonial times:

> they had no power saws, no earth-moving equipment, no trucks and cranes, and, at first, not even a horse or cart. They had their bare hands, a few axes, handsaws . . . wedges, mauls, picks, shovels, and hoes. With these implements they had to fell trees, shape timbers for their houses, rive [tear apart] clapboards and shingles, and erect their buildings. [The] amount of human toil required to establish themselves is hard for us even to imagine today.[6]

Two Spheres of Life

For decades, these hardy individuals living on farms near small rural villages on the edges of white civilization were on the cutting edge, so to speak, of American civilization. Some towns, especially on the coast, did steadily grow larger. But for a long time they retained many features of country life. Two centuries after New York City was founded in the 1600s, for example, pigs were still running loose in many parts of the city, consuming garbage people tossed out into the streets. And "it was a point of pride," Wright says, "for householders in towns to keep a milk cow" and "nearly every house had a vegetable garden. The day of the supermarket was still far in the [future]."[7]

Eventually, however, the largest towns, like New York, Boston, and Philadelphia, grew into big cities with few or no rural aspects. For farmers and other rural Americans, they seemed like distant places that were too noisy, crowded, and fast paced. They remained in a sense islands in the sea that was the larger wilderness of colonial America. And yet by the early to mid-1700s, those islands had come to influence the lives of the rural folk whether they liked it or not. True, the bulk of the population still dwelled in the countryside; everyday life on a colonial farm differed in numerous ways from life in a colonial city; and most city dwellers could not sustain themselves without the food produced in the hinterland. But

For the pilgrims, taming the wilderness was backbreaking labor.

at the same time, the cities remained the seats of government and the transmitters of the latest cultural ideas and customs. According to scholar John C. Miller, they "served as distributing centers for British and European culture." Miller says:

> The latest fashion, both in dress and ideas, reached the American people chiefly through the medium of the colonial seaports [and] they provided the best education available in the colonies. They [eventually] contained most of the educated men in British America. And they furnished a considerable part of the audience for plays, readers of the books and newspapers, and patrons of the arts.[8]

Thus, a sort of balance developed between the rural and urban spheres in colonial times. Various aspects of everyday life in each of these spheres depended to one degree or another on what happened in the other. Only much later, in the twentieth century, did average American customs and values become more homogenized and defined mainly by the urban sphere.

And yet, the memory of that largely agrarian, or agricultural, society of colonial times remains ingrained in the American psyche. Many modern Americans long for those days and hold onto the myth that America is largely made up of small towns and defined by small-town values. "Many Americans will not concede that an urban civilization" has replaced "the mores and habits of an agrarian state," Wright says, "and many political clichés carry over from the time when America was predominantly a nation of farmers."[9] This is undoubtedly one reason why a full two and a half centuries after the colonial era ended, Americans remain fascinated by the life and culture of their colonial past.

Chapter One

THE HOME AND ITS CONTENTS

The colonial American home was not merely a house, that is, a necessary shelter from the elements and a place to eat and sleep. It was also the abode of one of the primary colonial social units and institutions (along with the church and the government)—the family. Moreover, the colonial family itself was far more than simply a group of relatives sharing a house. Family members provided communication, human interaction, and support for one another and passed on their skills and values to their children. According to Louis B. Wright, an expert on colonial life, families

> stayed together for work and play in a way that is unknown now. In a period in which there were no labor-saving devices, mutual helpfulness was essential. When the daily chores were done, few external diversions lured the family to go its separate ways, as is our custom [today]. The family not only had to work together, but had to find amusements in which all could join. In the evening they might gather to hear someone read aloud, or they might listen to their elders telling stories. . . . The family might sing together or play games.[10]

Such activities, along with cooking, eating, home crafts, and sleeping, made a colonial house—itself little more than four walls and a roof—into a more dynamic and vibrant social unit, a true home.

Home life in British America varied somewhat from region to region, partly because of climate. Winters in New England were long and cold, for instance.

Clearing the Land

A majority of early settlers in the English colonies were farmers. And nearly all of them went through the difficult but necessary ritual of clearing tracts of land to create areas where they could plant crops. According to historians James M. Volo and Dorothy D. Volo:

Those considered the most able farmers cleared the land by cutting down all the trees in early summer, hauling off the valuable logs and leaving the least valuable wood and branches on the ground until the following spring. This was scavenged for firewood during the winter, and the leavings were burned in the early spring to complete the clearing. The burning left a layer of fine ash to fertilize and soften the ground between the remaining stumps. The stumps were usually allowed to rot of their own accord, but they could be pulled after a few years with the help of a team of oxen. Once the stumps were removed, the rocks and boulders could be dragged to the edges of the field on a sledge [a sledlike device] and dumped. In the winter, these stones could be made up into walls for the enclosure of sheep and cattle.

James M. Volo and Dorothy D. Volo, *Daily Life on the Old Colonial Frontier*, Westport, CT: Greenwood, 2002, p. 115.

This "dictated that the chimney should be placed in the center of the house," scholar John C. Miller writes in his book *The First Frontier: Life in Colonial America*. "The more indulgent [warmer] climate in the South made it possible to place the chimneys and fireplaces at the ends of the house."[11] Also, certain building materials were more prevalent in some areas than in others. Fieldstone was plentiful in New England, for example, whereas the scarcity of natural stone farther south caused people to turn more often to brick and other materials. The origin of the settlers was still another factor because they brought their customs with them when they crossed the Atlantic. And certain customs of home life differed from one part of Europe to another, and sometimes even from one part of England to another.

Erecting Houses

The manner in which houses were erected is a good example of how diverse such customs could be. In the initial years of settlement, most colonial houses looked roughly like the simple ones built at Jamestown in its first two decades. They were essentially small, one- or two-room medieval-like cottages with steep roofs made of thatch (bundles of dried straw or reeds) and walls of wattle (interwoven tree branches). The most common custom was to pack the wattle with mud to make it at least partially airtight.

The single or main room in such a house was called the "hall" or "keeping room." Cooking, eating, sleeping, and most other family activities took place there. If the house had a second room, it was usually called the "parlor." Here, there was a chance for privacy for certain activities, such as birthing children, courtship, or business meetings between the father and village elders.

In the initial first two decades of settlement, most colonial houses looked roughly like the simple ones built at Jamestown, seen here.

As new colonies expanded and prospered, more time and money could be devoted to erecting houses, which grew somewhat larger and more sturdy and permanent. Thatch and wattle were not only very impermant, but they were also highly flammable, so fires were common in early colonial villages. Plymouth's governor, William Bradford, almost died in such a fire in 1621. Eight years later Plymouth Colony banned thatched roofs, which were replaced by ones made of cedar shingles. And more and more New Englanders built their houses of fieldstones or wooden planks covered with shingles. By the late 1600s it was also common for houses to have a small kitchen, pantry, and bedroom in back of the hall, resulting in the so-called "saltbox" house.

Meanwhile, in the middle and southern colonies brick houses and log houses became very popular. The bricks were made from clay, which was plentiful in those colonies. After thoroughly mixing the clay with water, the colonists poured the mixture into wooden molds and allowed it to air-dry for a few weeks. Then they baked the molded clay for several days in large kilns containing multiple fires. For mortar (a substance used to fill the cracks between the bricks), it was common to mix lime (made from oyster shells) with sand.

Log cabins, later identified with American frontier heroes, such as Abraham Lincoln, were invented by the Swedes. A Dutch traveler named Jasper Danckaerts described a log cabin in colonial New Jersey in his journal in 1679. He writes:

Being made according to the Swedish mode, and as they usually build their houses here, [such cabins] are block-houses, being nothing else than entire trees, split through the middle, or squared out of the rough, and placed in the form of a square, upon each other, as high as they wish to have the house. The ends of these timbers are let [fitted] into each other, about a foot from the ends, half of one into half of the other. The whole structure is thus made without a nail or spike. . . . These houses are quite tight and warm.[12]

Whatever they were made of, none of the colonial houses had central heating. Instead, they had a fireplace that was not enough to heat the whole house, so people devised other ways to help stay warm. For example, German settlers in Pennsylvania and elsewhere used iron stoves that burned wood and vented the smoke through the house's chimney. Many colonists used a warming pan, a brass or copper container filled with embers from the fireplace, to warm the bed before bedtime. Using the pan's long handle, colonists slid the hot pan on and between the sheets, a little like a modern-day iron. Also, in the New Netherland Colony (later New York) many women warmed themselves in the winter with small pans filled with hot coals. According to a Swedish traveler who visited the colony in the 1600,

In colonial homes, the fireplace served many functions. Besides being the central gathering place in the home, it was also the heating system, the stove, and the lighting system.

it was customary for the women, all of them, even maidens, servants, and little girls, to put live coals into small iron pans which were in turn placed in a small stool resembling somewhat a footstool, but with a bottom [upon] which the pan was set. The top of the pan was full of holes, through which the heat came. They placed this stool with the warming pan under their skirts so that the [rising] heat [warmed them from the bottom up]. The women [had] spoiled themselves, for they could not do without this heat.[13]

Early Lighting Devices

Lighting in colonial houses, especially in the 1600s, was mostly poor. Windows were small and let in little light in the daytime. At night, the fire in the fireplace was the main source of interior light. Early settlers supplemented the firelight by burning pine knots (also called candlewood), made from thin slices of pine soaked in turpentine. They were burned in various places in the home, usually by placing them in small ceramic or metal containers, similar to how candles are used. Settlers also used small lamps that burned grease, fat, or oil. The most common was the "betty lamp," a metal container filled with grease that had a linen wick sticking out of one side. Such lamps could be hung from the ceiling or on walls with nails or hooks. Also widespread in early colonial houses were rushlights, made from the cores of river rushes that had been soaked in grease and allowed to harden. One drawback of these devices is that they smelled awful. Making traditional candles from tallow (animal fat) was at first rare because of the lack of farm animals. Even later, when sheep became plentiful, the candle-making process remained very time consuming. Eventually most people bought their candles from professional candle makers.

Evolving Furniture Fashions

In the colonies' early decades, most houses were sparsely furnished. Miller says, "So much had to be done—lands cleared, houses and barns built, wells dug—the settlers made do with the rudest sort of furniture."[14] Thus, there were no rugs, upholstered chairs, or pictures on the walls. There were also no closets. The general custom was to hang coats and other clothing items on pegs set into a board that was nailed to the wall.

Among the more common furniture items in early colonial homes were wooden tables and benches. Widely used was a "settle," a long bench with a narrow seat and a solid back to help protect sitters from cold drafts in the winter. Beds consisted of a simple wooden frame that held a straw-filled mattress; in poorer homes people often made do with a mattress alone. Linens, blankets, and clothing were stored in wooden chests.

Over time those colonists who could afford it, especially successful planters in the South and prosperous merchants in the North, obtained more extensive and better-quality furnishings. The walls of their houses sported wainscot paneling and hand-painted wallpaper imported from Europe. And carpets made in Turkey and other faraway lands covered the floors. The rooms were also filled with leather or banister-back chairs, finely made tables with wings that went up and down on hinges, and four-poster beds with elegant curtains hanging down to provide privacy and comfort. The mansions built by the richest colonists in the early to mid-1700s boasted even more varied and elegant furnishings. These were usually based on the latest fashions and trends from England and included fine walnut and mahogany chests of drawers, highboys and lowboys, and long dining tables, along with upholstered wing chairs covered in silks, brocades, and crewelwork (wool embroidery).

Food and Meals

Like the houses and their furnishings, the food eaten by the colonists varied over time and from place to place. At first, during the founding days of the settlements, corn was the major staple. Thanks to the local Indians, who showed them how to plant and prepare meals with corn, the colonists had access to a fast-growing, nutritious food source that

The furniture found in colonists' homes was typically wooden, sturdy, and functional.

required minimal labor to plant and harvest. And as time went on, the settlers created their own corn-based recipes. These included spoon bread (a pudding-like bread), johnnycake (flat bread made from cornmeal), and Indian pudding (a baked custard containing milk, eggs, and molasses). Another common colonial corn dish was samp, a hot porridge made by pounding corn with wooden or stone implements and boiling it.

As the early colonies expanded, so did the variety of foods in the colonists' diet. Other crops that became common in colonial gardens and fields included squashes, pumpkins, peas, chestnuts, and strawberries. In addition, blackberries, blueberries, acorns, and dandelion greens could be found growing in profusion in the wild. The settlers also happily found that wild game was plentiful. Deer, geese, ducks, wild turkeys, rabbits, pigeons, and other animals provided protein for those who took the time to go hunting. The meat was used in stews or roasted over spits, either in the fireplace or over an outdoor fire. To add flavor to both meat and vegetable dishes, the settlers had to rely on imported spices. Salt came from Spain, among other places; sugar from the Caribbean islands; and other spices from the Far East (via Dutch traders).

For beverages, the colonists at first drank those they were used to. Late medieval and early modern Britons loved beer and ale. And it was common for members of colonial families—including the children—to drink a cup of ale every morning. Over time, however, the colonists learned to enjoy many different types of drinks. In his advertisements designed to draw new settlers to Pennsylvania, that colony's founder, William Penn, included the following description of the local beverages:

> Our drink has been beer and punch, made of rum and water. Our beer was mostly made of molasses, which, well-boiled with sassafras and pine [resin] infused in it, makes [a] very tolerable drink. But now they make malt, and malt drink begins to be common. . . . In our great town [Philadelphia], there is an able man who has set up a large brew house in order to furnish the people with good drink.[15]

Mealtimes varied across the colonies depending on the colonists' local habits and schedules. Some people ate breakfast early, right after they awakened, while others went out and worked for a while, then returned home and ate breakfast in late morning. It was also quite common in many colonies to eat a large meal (supper) in the late afternoon and then a smaller one or a snack in the evening just before going to bed.

Among the various aspects of colonial mealtimes, the table manners of that era seem the strangest to modern eyes. Men regularly wore their hats at the table, for instance, while younger children stood rather than sat at the table while eating. It was also customary for two people to share the same plate—most often a trencher, a block of wood with a bowl-like area carved out of the center. Any family in which each person had his or her own separate trencher was seen as putting on airs. Also during the 1600s, most people ate food with their fingers, except for soups and porridges that were eaten with spoons. Forks did not become common in the colonies until the 1700s.

Finally, leftovers from one meal were often served at the next meal. This was

A homemaker roasts a pig over the fire in the central fireplace.

"not merely a matter of thrift," historians James M. Volo and Dorothy D. Volo explain. "Prior to refrigeration, there was no safe way to save extra portions for a later date."[16] Nevertheless, the colonists did employ some rudimentary ways of preserving some foods. Carrots, radishes, potatoes, and some other vegetables could be stored in root cellars, where it was cool, for weeks. Corn, beans, and peas could be preserved by drying them. And fruits could be made into pureed sauces, like apple butter, that lasted longer than the fresh fruits themselves. In addition, pork (which eventually became a mainstay of the colonial diet) and other meats could be preserved for a few months by salting, smoking, or pickling them.

Other Activities

Not only were colonial homes places for cooking, eating, sleeping, and taking refuge from the rain, cold, and other elements, but they were also places for a diverse array of other activities. Some were social in nature. Family members (and sometimes one or more neighbors) regularly told stories, listened to one member read the Bible or other books, sang songs, talked about the latest news, or prayed together.

But many other activities, especially in early colonial times, involved making items that were necessary for the family's survival and/or comfort. It was common to make soap in the home, for instance. According to a noted expert on colonial life:

Mealtime Rules for Children

According to Alice M. Earle, a prolific writer about colonial American life, mealtime rules for children were often extremely strict. In her book Home Life in Colonial Days, *Earle writes:*

[Children] were to eat in silence, as fast as possible (regardless of indigestion), and leave the table as speedily as might be. . . . They were ordered never to seat themselves at the table until after the blessing had been asked and their parents told them to be seated. They were never to ask for anything on the table; never to speak unless spoken to; always to break the bread, not to bite into a whole slice; never to take salt except with a clean knife; [and] not to throw bones under the table. . . . One rule [was] "Look not earnestly at any other person that is eating." When children had eaten all that had been given them . . . they were told to leave at once the table and room.

Alice M. Earle, *Home Life in Colonial Days*, Teddington, England: Echo Library, 2009, pp. 102–103.

A common household activity for female colonists was making their own soap, a time-consuming, messy chore.

to the accompaniment of a ghastly odor, grease and lye were boiled together in big iron kettles, out in the open air. The mess was constantly stirred and it cooked into a harsh, soft soap. For some reason the operation wasn't always successful, and it was hence a courtesy to wish a neighbor luck with her soap.[17]

Many colonists also made barrels by hollowing out fat logs. This could be done with knives and other hand tools, a long and laborious process; but many people came to use fire, a technique borrowed from the Indians (who hollowed out logs to make canoes that way). Other common items that the colonists made include spoons, trenchers, bowls, and shovels (called spades) by carving them from wood. In these and other ways, homes in British colonial America were almost constantly the scenes of hard work and industry, traits that were essential in creating a new civilization from scratch.

Chapter Two

Women, Courtship, and Marriage

The lives of women in colonial America, especially in its first several decades, were in some ways like a coin with two very different sides. On the positive side, colonial mothers and wives often had more weighty responsibilities and more freedom of choice, both in the home and in society, than most European women of that era did. As a result, colonial women were very efficient at running their homes. And they were often indispensable as helpmates to their husbands, fathers, and society in general. Historical records are replete with stories of women who ran the home and sometimes the family business for months or even years while their husbands were away. For example, in a letter to his wife, Deborah, in 1757 colonial inventor and politician Benjamin Franklin wrote, "I leave home and undertake this long voyage [to Europe]

more cheerful, as I can rely on your prudence in the management of my affairs, and [the] education of my dear child."[18] And in the late 1600s noted Massachusetts judge Samuel Sewall recorded in his diary: "Gave my wife the rest of my cash [and told] her she shall now keep the cash. If I want, I will borrow of her. She has a better facility than I at managing affairs. I will assist her."[19]

On the negative side was the fact that with very rare exceptions, one of them Samuel Sewall, men considered women to be inferior to men, especially intellectually and morally. It was not a coincidence that men ran society and excluded women from voting and taking part in government. Simply put, the general male view was that women lacked the "smarts" to do such things. In 1645 Massachusetts leader John Winthrop sternly criticized a woman for "meddling" in men's affairs for the "offense" of becoming highly literate. In his journal he wrote,

> [The wife of] the governor of [Connecticut] was fallen into a sad infirmity, the loss of her understanding and reason, which had been growing upon her diverse years, by occasion of her giving herself wholly to reading and writing, and had written many books. Her husband, being very loving and tender of her, was loath to grieve her; but he saw his error when it was too late. For if she had attended her household affairs and such things as belong to women, and not gone out of her way and calling to meddle in such things as are proper for men, whose minds are stronger, etc., she had kept her wits and might have improved them usefully and honorably in the place God had set her.[20]

"From Sunrise to Long After Sunset"

The place "God had set" for women, according to colonial men, was in and around the home. And that is where the vast majority of colonial women toiled away their lives. These women were called on to exhibit what today would be seen as extraordinary discipline, patience, and sheer physical strength and endurance. One expert writes, "The labor of the colonial housewife was back-breaking drudgery," and

in a frontier settlement, housekeeping was only part of her duties. She helped to clear the land and build the house and plant the crops as well. Even when she lived in a village of snug, comfortable houses, her daily tasks filled every hour from sunrise to long after sunset.[21]

This portrait of women's lives filled with seemingly relentless duties and work began at the very inception of the colonies in the early 1600s. The few women aboard the *Mayflower* and other ships carrying the initial settlers cut down trees, built houses, and tilled the soil right along with their menfolk, as well as bore and raised the children, cooked, and cleaned—all this quite often while underfed and ill from a host of ailments. It is no wonder that life expectancy was low in those days (average life expectancy was in the thirties and forties, whereas today's is in the seventies), for both men and women but especially for the women, who often simply worked themselves to death. Modern experts estimate that the chances of both a colonial husband and wife surviving more than ten years of marriage together in the 1600s was only one in three! According to one noted American writer, generations of these early American women "sank at last into nameless graves, without any vision of the grateful days when millions of their descendants should rise up and call themselves blessed."[22]

One way to appreciate the load that colonial women carried, especially in

With no mechanical or electrical devices to ease her burden, a colonial woman's daily housekeeping chores were physically demanding. Here, a woman is shown churning her own butter.

the colonies' early years, is to compare their duties to those of modern women. Many modern American women cook, clean, and raise their children, as well as hold down jobs. But they do not make all the family clothes from scratch, make candles to light the home, make soap to keep the family clean, make quilts to keep everyone warm, or prepare a large proportion of the food for the winter in advance. Elizabeth G. Speare, a noted writer about colonial times, describes the last of these duties:

Autumn was the busiest time of all for the housewife, and for the children as well, for every pair of hands was needed to make ready for the winter. Quinces [a fruit that looks like a yellow apple], pears, plums, peaches, and berries of all sorts were preserved in huge crocks or boiled into rich spicy jams and marmalades. Apples were peeled and sliced and strung up to dry for winter pies, or boiled in the kettles to make vast barrels of applesauce or apple butter. Meat and fish were salted down or smoked and packed into barrels. Cheese was pressed into flat wheels. In addition, a housewife prided herself on a store of fancy pickles and relishes, made from such unlikely plants as nasturtium buds, green walnuts, barberries, marigolds, roses, violets, and peonies.[23]

In addition to the everyday chores of cooking, cleaning, making clothes, and other tasks, colonial women were responsible for raising the children. Families of ten or more children were common at this time.

As if these many and varied duties were not enough, women also had to carry and bear the children. In an age when the causes of disease were not yet known and the state of medicine fairly primitive, infant mortality was high. A whopping four out of ten children born in colonial America died before the age of six. As a result, it was common for couples to have seven, ten, twelve, or even fifteen or more children. This created for many women a "cycle of pregnancy, birth, and nursing that set the bounds of [their lives] for the remainder of [their] childbearing years,"[24] according to Volo and Volo. The physical strain of multiple pregnancies alone took a huge toll on colonial women. In addition to their long list of other duties, therefore, women also had to keep constant watch over a large brood of offspring while preparing for the next birthing experience.

Such childbirths took place in the home. It was customary for a midwife from the local community to oversee the event, aided by several of the expectant mother's female family members and friends. In addition to these individuals, the husband, other children (if any), and other invited guests were in and out of the house during her labor. All of them had to be fed. And incredibly, this added responsibility was also laid on the woman. Just before giving birth she was expected to prepare large amounts of food for her company and family.

Courtship Customs

Women were also involved in, and quite often the center of attention in, the rituals of courtship. In general courtship in colonial America was ritualized and formal—very different from modern-day dating. First, there was very little privacy in colonial homes and communities, which meant that there was almost nowhere for a young woman and the young man courting her to spend time alone. One way around this dilemma was the widely accepted practice of "bundling." With the girl's parents (and presumably other family members) sitting in the same room, the boy and girl climbed into a bed fully clothed. They then snuggled under the sheets and whispered private words for as long as they were allowed, after which the boy departed.

Bundling was popular across most of the colonies for much of the colonial period. And a number of authors mention it, often positively, in both poems and prose. One of the poems reads:

Some maidens say, if through the nation bundling should quite go out of fashion, courtship would lose its sweets; and they could have no fun till wedding day. It shan't be so, they rage and storm, and country girls in clusters swarm, and fly and buzz, like angry bees, and vow they'll bundle when they please. Some mothers too, will plead their cause, and give their daughters great applause, and tell them, 'tis no sin nor shame, for we, your mothers, did the same.[25]

Bundling did "go out of fashion" in the 1750s and 1760s, however, mainly because several influential clergymen began calling it a sin.

In colonial America most marriages were arranged by parents, especially the father, who was usually the head of the household. He tended to be more concerned that his daughter marry a man with money and social position than someone she loved. In 1764 a Virginia man named Bernard Moore was delighted to hear assurances of monetary support in a letter from John Walker, the father of a young man who wanted to marry Moore's daughter. Walker wrote:

I think myself able to afford for their support in case of a union. . . . I will promise one thousand [English] pounds to be paid in the year 1765, and one thousand pounds to be paid in the year 1766; and the further sum of two thousand pounds I promise to give him. . . . The above sums are all to be in money or lands.[26]

In fact, money was a factor on both sides. Whatever funds the groom brought to the marriage were amplified by the dowry the young woman's father supplied at the outset. A dowry is money or other valuables provided

Women Should Be Subject to Men

In his journal John Winthrop, a leading Massachusetts colonist, states the prevailing male view about women during colonial times, namely that men should exert extensive control over women. Winthrop writes:

The woman's own choice makes such a man her husband, yet being so chosen, he is her lord and she is to be subject to him, yet in a way of liberty, not of bondage, and a true wife accounts her subjection, her honor, and freedom, and would not think her condition safe and free but in her subjection to her husband's authority. Such is the liberty of the church under the authority of Christ, her king and husband. His yoke is so easy and sweet to her as a bride's ornaments. And if through forwardness and wantonness, etc., she shake it [her husband's authority] off at any time, she is at no rest in her spirit until she take it up again. And whether her lord smiles upon her and embraces her in his arms, or rebukes [rejects] or smites [strikes] her, she apprehends the sweetness of his love.

John Winthrop, *Winthrop's Journal, "History of New England," 1630–1649*, vol. 2, ed., James Kendall Hosmer, New York: Scribner's, 1908, p. 239.

Hardships Faced by Single Women

Many of the single women who traveled to the colonies in the early to mid-1600s were indentured servants. In his book Everyday Life in Early America, *historian David F. Hawke discusses some of the problems they faced. He writes:*

[A single woman] was obliged to serve out her indenture, and since the law forbade a servant to marry until she had completed her contract, that meant four or five years must pass before she could get a husband. They were devastating years. Exposure to malaria left her susceptible to more deadly diseases. The physical work was harder than anything she had known in England. If she served a small planter, she had, in addition to household chores, the fields to tend. She was easily exploited and degraded, for on an isolated farm there were few effective checks to the authority of the planter or his often shrewish wife. . . . If the woman lived through her service, a quick marriage was inevitable in a land where men outnumbered women seven to one.

David F. Hawke, *Everyday Life in Early America*, New York: Harper and Row, 1989, pp. 63–64.

to the groom by a bride's parents for her maintenance during her marriage. And because colonial American men controlled their family finances, a new husband had direct access to the dowry money after the wedding.

But first, the prospective groom was expected to ask a young woman's father for permission to marry her. And if the father did not give that permission, the odds were that the marriage would not take place. Still, a few independent-minded young women had the courage to stand up to their fathers and choose their husbands themselves. One was a South Carolinian, Eliza Lucas, who in the late 1730s turned down two suitors chosen by her father, a British military officer. In a letter she wrote to him when he was away at war, she said:

As you propose Mr. L. to me [as a possible husband], I am sorry I can't have sentiments favorable enough to him to take time to think on the subject. . . . As I know 'tis my happiness you consult, I must beg the favor of you to pay my compliments to the old gentleman for his generosity and favorable sentiments of me and let him know my thoughts [on this matter]. As to the other gentleman you mention, Mr. W., you know sir that I have so slight a knowledge of him, I can form no judgment [of him]. But give me leave to assure you my dear sir that a single life is my only choice—and if it were not as I am yet but eighteen, I hope you will put aside the thoughts of my marrying yet these [next] two or three years at least.[27]

"Plain, Simple, and Unadorned"

Whether they chose marital partners as directed by their fathers or made their own choices, almost all colonial women (and men, too) eventually did get married. This simple fact of life was driven by the realities of society at that time. Volo and Volo explain, "Marriage

Like colonial life in general, weddings, as shown here, were basic and simple.

Widowhood in the Colonies

In colonial society a man was the dominant member of his family, through which legitimacy and notoriety passed from father to son. So when a man died, his wife was seen merely as a sort of sad leftover from a union that no longer existed. Still, in most colonies a widow had the legal right to inherit a substantial part of her husband's estate. She usually received one-third of the household goods and one-third of the income from the family lands until such time as she remarried. Still, at the insistence of other family members, local courts sometimes appointed a male family member to manage the estate, assuming a man could do this more efficiently. Becoming a widow often put a woman in control of her life and money for the first time in her life, and some were reluctant to remarry and lose that control to a new husband. Many widows, however, did get married again. Others remained single and went to live in the households of their married adult children. As members of extended families, they were often welcomed because they provided an extra pair of hands to do the many household tasks.

was presumed for all adult men and women," and

there simply was no acceptable place for sexual expression outside of marriage. This was particularly true in New England, where legal as well as religious authority prohibited any extramarital sexual activity. Communities feared that unwed mothers would not be able to provide for themselves and would ultimately be a drain on the community.[28]

Under these conditions, women who got pregnant before marriage had no choice but to marry immediately. (This was not rare; an estimated 20 percent of colonial maidens were already with child when they got married.)

As for the wedding ceremony itself, it was a rather bleak and dull affair by today's standards. According to scholar John C. Miller:

there was no wedding dress, no throwing of rice, no bridesmaids, music, ring, prayers, or benediction. The couple simply clasped hands before a magistrate [public official] and heard themselves pronounced man and wife, a fitting introduction to life in colonial New England: plain, simple, and unadorned.[29]

Chapter Three

CHILDREN AND EDUCATION

Childhood in colonial America was very different from childhood in modern America. First, the average number of children per family or household was much higher than it is today. Most modern couples have one, two, or three children, and families with seven or eight children are considered unusually large.

In colonial times seven or eight children per household was common. And families with more than ten children were not deemed at all remarkable. William Phips, governor of the Massachusetts Bay Colony from 1692 to 1694, came from a family with twenty-six children. A Virginia man named Robert Carter had seventeen children. And the famous inventor and politician Benjamin Franklin also came from a household with seventeen children. With such large families, a mere handful of couples could, over the

course of a few generations, populate an entire town or county. For example, a New England woman who died in 1742 left behind sixty-one grandchildren and 182 great-grandchildren.

One reason that colonial families had so many children and grandchildren was that infant mortality rates were much higher than they are now. Thus, many couples had large numbers of children in case several of those offspring died in infancy or childhood. An even more important reason was the desperate need for cheap labor. Carving farms and villages out of the wilderness and maintaining them was extremely difficult and time consuming. And the more young boys there were to help with the planting and harvesting, and the more young girls there were to do housework and milk the cows, the better. In addition, most colonists felt that large families

An Impressive Writing Ability

When they were old enough to read and write, many colonial children wrote letters, including some to parents who were away from home. The following letter was penned by John Quincy Adams to his father, the famous lawyer and patriot John Adams. Considering that the boy was ten years old at the time, it demonstrates the impressive writing ability and devotion to learning of the better-educated young colonists.

Dear Sir: I love to receive letters very well, much better than I love to write them. I make but a poor figure at composition. My head is much too fickle. My thoughts are running after birds eggs, play, and trifles until I get vexed with myself. I have but just entered the 3rd vol. of [the works of Scottish author Tobias] Smollett, tho' I had designed to have got it half through by this time. I have determined this week to be more diligent. . . . If I can keep but my resolution, I will write again at the end of the week and give a better account of myself. I wish, Sir, you would give me some instructions with regard to my time & advise me how to proportion my studies and my play. In writing, I will keep them by me & endeavor to follow them.

Quoted in John T. Morse, *John Quincy Adams*, Boston: Houghton Mifflin, 1898, pp. 3–4.

were warranted because there was plenty of land available to support them. The general view was that God had provided enough space and potential food supplies to support inordinate numbers of people. According to scholar John C. Miller:

Americans seemed to have assumed that they had been specially commissioned to replenish the Earth and that no time could be lost in accomplishing this mission. . . . On the Carolina frontier, every cabin contained ten or twelve young children [and] often the children and grandchildren of the same couple were of the same age. Uncles and nephews, aunts and nieces all frolicked together in the mud. The Indians could have read their doom in the census figures.[30]

A Sin to Play

Another characteristic of childhood in colonial America was that it was relatively short and significantly less carefree and joyful than childhood is today. First, what is now seen as the second half of childhood—adolescence—did not exist in colonial times. By the time boys and girls reached the age of twelve or thirteen, they were expected to act like and to assume practically the same responsibilities as adults.

Moreover, even the early years of childhood were often stern and cheerless by modern standards. Willfulness and playfulness, today seen as normal childhood traits, were then viewed as unhealthy, even sinful. In his diary, Massachusetts judge Samuel Sewall wrote that while he was cleaning out the downspout on the corner of his house,

In colonial times, when a child reached the age of 12 or 13 he or she was considered an adult. Normal childhood playfulness, even among the youngest of children, was not tolerated.

he found a ball lodged inside. Realizing that his son had hidden it there, he called for a minister and the two men lectured the child for hours, telling him that it was a sin to play. The devil and other powers of darkness constantly tempted children into such frivolous activities, they said, and the boy must learn to resist the temptation to play. That way he could avoid falling into wickedness. In the New England colonies, many parents required three- and four-year-olds to memorize the following lines from a children's catechism (a book of religious principles): "Question: What must become of you if you are wicked? Answer: I shall be sent down to everlasting fire and hell among wicked and miserable creatures."[31]

It was usually not enough to make children memorize and recite such tracts, however. Children naturally felt the urge to play and question the world around them, and most adults believed such tendencies had to be suppressed, if necessary by physical means. One Pilgrim minister said in a sermon, "Surely there is in all children . . . a stubbornness and stoutness of mind arising from natural pride, which must in the first place be broken and beaten down."[32] Beatings were quite common in most households (as well as in schools) and were administered with all manner of tools. Rods and switches cut from birches and other trees were widely used. Some parents and teachers tied leather straps to the end of a stick, creating a whip sometimes called a tattling stick. Still another means of punishment was the flapper, described by one

expert on colonial life as "a heavy piece of leather six inches in diameter, with a hole in the middle. This was fastened by an edge to a pliable handle. Every stroke on the bare flesh raised a blister the size of the hole in the leather."[33]

One reason that so many adults felt it necessary to beat playfulness and other "immorality" out of children was that they had once been children themselves. Many grownups still sometimes felt such playful urges, equated them with sin, and regretted that they had not been punished enough as children; hence they felt the need to make sure their own children were properly cleansed of wickedness. Apparently it occurred to very few, if any, adults that they were simply perpetuating a cycle of abuse and misery from one generation to the next.

With such attitudes about childhood and play in force, it is not surprising that most of a colonial child's waking, nonschool hours were spent doing chores. A preacher named Henry Ward Beecher wrote how when he was a boy he had to wake up every morning before dawn and build the kitchen fire. In winter, if it had snowed, he had to dig a tunnel through the snow to reach the woodpile. He also had to feed the horses and cows and fetch water for the house, all before setting out for school. In the evenings, after school, he spent hours doing other household chores. Meanwhile, little girls sometimes helped their brothers and fathers in the fields. But more often they helped their mothers comb wool, spin yarn, knit stockings,

The Sins of His Youth

Many colonial children were brought up in strictly religious fashion. Some, especially among the early Puritans, feared God's wrath for the least offense. And even later, as adults, they remained filled with remorse for sins they had committed in childhood. One was Massachusetts reverend Nathaniel Mather, who wrote:

When very young I went astray from God and my mind was altogether taken with vanities and follies, such as the remembrance of them does greatly abuse my soul within me. Of the manifold [numerous] sins which then I was guilty of, none so sticks upon me, as that, being very young, I was whittling on the Sabbath Day [Sunday], and for fear of being seen, I did it behind the door. [This was] a great reproach of God!, a specimen of that atheism I brought into the world with me.

Quoted in Arthur W. Calhoun, *A Social History of the American Family*, vol. 1, Cleveland, OH: Clark, 1917, p. 110.

---

weave shoelaces and belts, mend torn clothes, cook, and clean.

Some parents, especially in later colonial times when harsh attitudes about childhood began to relax a little, did allow their children to play with toys, but only briefly and when their daily chores were completed. Most such toys were handmade, either by the children themselves or by other family members. In the 1700s there were a few professional toy makers in the larger cities, like Boston and Philadelphia, but children in the countryside rarely had access to their products. Common toys for boys included balls made from cloth covered in sheepskin, whistles carved from willow branches, wooden tops, hoops made from barrel tops, and kites. As remains true today, little girls enjoyed dolls. Eliz-abeth G. Speare, a noted writer about colonial times, writes:

There were corncob dolls and braided cornhusk dolls with their silky hair, and rag dolls with indigo-painted eyes and berry-red mouths. . . . Indulgent [generous] fathers and grandfathers made doll-sized cradles and chairs. Occasionally a fortunate child possessed a tiny set of dishes, pewter or china, imported from England.[34]

Early Schools and Learning

Today it is taken for granted that children attend school regularly until they are about eighteen years old. In colonial America, however, this was rarely

Unlike schools of today, in colonial times children of all ages were educated together in a one-room schoolhouse.

the case. First, there were no schools in the earliest colonial decades. A few, small, private schools appeared in the Massachusetts Bay Colony in the late 1630s and early 1640s. And from 1647 on, Massachusetts required by law that towns with fifty or more families had to provide a school that was open to all children in that town.

The main reason that Massachusetts stressed education was that its founders, the Puritans, were big believers in learning. They viewed it essential that a godly person be able to read the Bible. Hence, a certain level of reading and writing ability had to be attained by both boys and girls.

The so-called grammar schools these children attended taught them basic reading and spelling, along with some rudimentary arithmetic. The schoolhouses were generally one-room structures in which students of all ages attended class together. The teacher sat behind a desk on a raised platform and instructed the pupils, who sat on wooden benches, in their ABCs and how to copy sentences from texts variously called hornbooks, readers, and copybooks. Josiah Quincy, who eventually became a renowned Massachusetts educator, learned by such rote copying in a grammar school at age six. He recall:

I was compelled to sit with four other boys on the same hard bench daily [and] study lessons which I could not understand . . . the rule being that there should be no advance until the first book was conquered. I kept in [that first book] I know not how long. All I know is, I must have gone over it twenty times before mastering it.[35]

Although education was mandatory in Massachusetts, one did not have to attend one of the formal schools to abide by the law. There were a number of alternative routes to learning, one of which was for parents to teach their children at home. Those parents who could afford

The Hard Life of a Teacher

Many colonial teachers, or schoolmasters, were dedicated and hardworking, but made little money. Elizabeth G. Speare, a noted writer about colonial times, discusses their often difficult lives in her book Life in Colonial America. *She writes:*

His life was not an easy one. To qualify as schoolmaster, a young man needed a stout heart more than vast learning. His wages were low and uncertain, paid in corn, turnips, onions, firewood, or other produce. Though his desk was nearest the fire, the green wood with which parents paid their sons' tuitions did not always give off enough heat to thaw the ink frozen in the inkpot. He had to keep control all day of an explosive roomful of boys who were likely to retaliate with tricks such as stuffing the chimney and smoking him out. [And] he must have spent his evenings setting out the lines to be copied [by the students] the next morning. Yet there were gifted teachers who ruled their classes with gentleness and earned the undying loyalty of their boys.

Elizabeth G. Speare, *Life in Colonial America*, New York: Random House, 1963, p. 108.

it hired tutors or sent their children to England to be educated. There were also old-friend schools; these were informal, temporary learning sessions overseen by roving teachers who worked for small fees paid by parents. Another alternative was a dame school. It consisted of a group of eight to ten young boys and girls who gathered in the kitchen (or another room) of a local woman's home. These teachers, the "dames," taught only the basics, often to prepare the children for more formal schooling to come.

In still another educational route, a number of colonists became educated mainly by teaching themselves. Books of various kinds, especially those containing religious stories and sermons and some on law, military affairs, and medicine, were available in the early colonies. And some people took full advantage of them. Benjamin Franklin, for instance, learned some basics of reading and writing in a brief stint in a grammar school, then taught himself the rest by reading. In his autobiography, he writes:

From my infancy, I was passionately fond of reading, and all the little money that came into my hands was laid out in the purchasing of books. . . . My father's little library consisted chiefly of books in [religious topics], most of which I read. . . . There were [also] among them [the ancient Greek biographer] Plutarch's Lives, in which I read abundantly, and I still think that time spent to great advantage.[36]

Education was mandated by law in the Massachusetts Bay Colony, but was less emphasized in the mid-Atlantic and southern colonies.

Harvard College, shown here in 1638, was established by Puritan leaders in the Massachusetts Bay Colony.

Outside of New England, less emphasis was placed on education at first. In part this was because many colonial leaders did not value education as highly as the Puritans did. Also, populations in most of the mid-Atlantic and southern colonies were more spread out, making it difficult for students from a given region to gather in a single classroom or school. For the most part, fewer people in these areas became educated. And those who did learned in church schools, a few select private schools, or from their parents.

Higher Education

Another area in which New England led the way was higher education. In 1636

when the Massachusetts Bay Colony was still small and no formal town schools yet existed, the colony's leaders founded Harvard College, the first institution of higher learning in British America. One colonist described it seven years later:

After God had carried us safe to New England, and we had built our houses . . . reared convenient places for God's worship, and settled the civil government, one of the next things we longed for and looked after was to advance learning and perpetuate it to posterity. [And] as we were thinking and consulting how to effect this great work, it pleased God to stir up the heart of one Mr. Harvard [to] give the one half of his estate [toward] the erecting of a college, and all his library. After him another [colonist] gave 300 [English pounds], others after them cast in more, and the public hand of the state added the rest. The college . . . is called (according to the name of the first founder) Harvard College.[37]

Harvard rapidly came to teach a fulsome curriculum, including grammar, logic, Latin, Greek, Hebrew, mathematics, and astronomy. The students—for a long time male only—at first lived in small rooms, each equipped only with a hard bed, a storage chest, and a pitcher and basin for washing up. There were no school-sponsored sports. Recreation consisted of informal swimming in the Charles River or skating on it in the winter. There was also a strict dress code. It read in part, "No scholar shall go out of his chamber without coat, gown, or cloak, and everyone everywhere shall wear modest and sober habit [dress] without strange ruffian-like or newfangled fashions."[38]

Later, some of the other colonies established their own colleges. The College of William and Mary opened in Virginia in the 1690s; Yale University started in Connecticut in the early 1700s; Princeton University was founded in 1746 in New Jersey; and Columbia University appeared in New York in 1754. Today these and other colonial American institutions remain among the finest universities in the world, a testament to the strong spirit of learning instilled in some of America's earliest pioneers.

Chapter Four

OCCUPATIONS, WORK, AND TECHNOLOGY

The English and other settlers who crossed the Atlantic to North America in the 1600s naturally had to find ways of making a living. A majority of them tried their hand at farming, including many who had not been farmers in Europe. And although the colonists pursued a great many crafts and other professions, for many decades agriculture remained the most prevalent occupation and form of work in British America.

The colonists' general approach to farming differed from the one long used in Europe. In the Old World, fertile land was increasingly scarce, especially when measured against the large and ever-growing population. So farmers were always looking for ways to maintain or improve the productivity of the existing soil. In America, by contrast, there were very few people (even counting the Indi-

ans) and huge amounts of arable land. So most early colonists adopted a wasteful approach. According to eighteenth-century traveler Pehr Kalm:

the Europeans coming to America found a rich, fine soil before them [and] they had nothing to do but cut down the wood . . . and to clear the dead leaves away. They could then immediately proceed to plowing, which in such loose ground is very easy. And having sown their grain, they got a most plentiful harvest. This easy method of getting a rich crop has spoiled the [settlers], and induced them to . . . sow uncultivated grounds as long as they will produce a crop without manuring, but to turn them into pastures as soon as they can bear no more, and to take on new spots of ground. . . .

Farming was the most prevalent occupation in colonial America for many decades.

Their eyes are fixed upon the present gain, and they are blind to the future.[39]

Kalm and other observers note that only the German settlers avoided this form of soil exhaustion and instead practiced crop rotation (growing crops in one field while the one next to it is left empty and allowed to rebuild its nutrients, and then reversing the situation the next growing season). It is important to point out, however, that no one yet had a scientific explanation for why crop rotation was more effective and economical. And the irony is that when such explanations did come, it was mainly Americans who advanced them. In 1748 a Connecticut preacher and farmer named Jared Elliot published *Essays on Field-Husbandry in New England*. Attempting to apply scientific ideas to agriculture, he suggested that soil fertility was dependent mostly on the organic matter it contained. And he showed that certain crops and fertilizers could rebuild depleted soil. This was only one of many technological advances made by the early colonists that contributed to the rise of science in both America and Europe.

Masters and Apprentices

While colonial villages and the countryside surrounding them were the domain of farmers, the towns and cities were populated mainly by nonfarmers who practiced a number of useful skills and crafts. Many of these crafts and occupations employed the apprentice system. In this system an established, skilled professional—the master—took in and over time trained an unskilled young person—the apprentice. There were two general types of apprenticeship. One was when a child's parents offered the child to the master, who lodged and fed as well as trained him or her; the other was when town officials assigned orphaned or abandoned children to one or more masters.

In many ways, an apprentice was like an indentured servant. His or her parents signed a contract with the master. That document stipulated that the young person would live and train with the master for a set number of years. The average was four or five years, unless the apprentice ran away before finishing the term of service. Running away was actually fairly common. Benjamin Franklin was apprenticed to a printer (his older brother James) at age twelve and ran away when he was seventeen. He recalls:

Long-Distance Vehicles and Roads

Wainwrights, or wagon makers, were vital in colonial days. In his book Colonial Living, *Edwin Tunis, a noted authority on colonial life, discusses the wagons then used to haul goods and passengers overland and the roads that carried them. Tunis writes:*

The Pennsylvania Germans evolved the great Conestoga wagon to serve the western trade and also to haul their own farm products down to tidewater. These wagons were . . . high and heavy and extremely strong. [The] larger wagons were drawn by eight horses. [Later, small coaches that carried passengers came into use.] The "waggoners" camped at night, feeding their horses from a long trough. [Over time] life grew a little more comfortable for the wagon men as the roads improved from sheer use and crude inns were opened along them. The streets of town along the coast were extended to become local roads. [More land was cleared for roads in inland regions. But] "clearing" meant cutting trees. Such things as boulders, stumps, and mud holes were left as they stood. A coach driver always carried an ax to clear obstructions, and his male passengers were called upon to push when necessary.

Edwin Tunis, *Colonial Living*, Baltimore: Johns Hopkins University Press, 1999, pp. 119–120.

I concluded [decided] to remove [myself] to New York [from Boston]. But my father now siding with my brother, I was sensible that if I attempted to go openly, means would be made to prevent me. My friend Collins, therefore, [helped me escape]. He agreed with the captain of a New York sloop to take me [and I] was taken on board the sloop privately [and] in three days found my self in New York, near three hundred miles from my home . . . without the least recommendation or knowledge of any person in the place, and very little money in my pocket.[40]

One reason that apprentices ran away is that many lacked either the interest or aptitude, or both, to perform their master's trade. So even a number of those who stayed and served out their terms of service did not end up in the occupation, or if they did, they did not do well in it. On the flip side, however, some apprentices did have the aptitude required. They went on to become full-fledged assistants (journeymen) and eventually masters themselves.

A woodworker shows a young apprentice his tools and techniques.

Barrel makers played a key role in colonial American society. Barrels were used for storing numerous everyday products, such as gunpowder and grain, and as such were in high demand.

Essential Professionals

Whether they had apprentices or not, craftsmen and other workers in the towns, and in some villages, too, played essential roles in the socioeconomic system that allowed the colonies to thrive and grow. On the one hand, the farmers supplied the food for both themselves and the nonfarmers. On the other, the craftsmen and other professionals supplied various goods and services that the farmers lacked either the time or expertise to produce.

The cooper, or barrel maker, was a good example. There was a huge need for barrels and other similar storage containers in colonial America. In the southern colonies, in fact, making such containers was the second-largest profession next to farming. The barrels a cooper constructed were used for storing grain, cornmeal, flour, maple syrup, beer, cider, molasses, salted meat or fish, rum, gunpowder, and hundreds of other everyday products. Coopers also made pails for carrying water and washtubs for doing laundry.

How Mail Got Through

Mail carriers and postal workers did not exist in colonial times because there was no official postal service. Instead, someone who wanted to send a letter long distance gave it to a traveler who was headed in the general direction. The traveler might be going overland by foot, horse, or wagon. Or he or she might take a boat along the coast or a river. If the traveler changed direction during the trip, he might leave the letter at an inn. There it might sit for a while until another traveler going in the right direction picked it up. It therefore frequently took a couple of months or more for a letter to go only a few hundred miles.

A typical letter was written in ink on paper, if the writer could afford it, but if not, on a piece of linen. Because envelopes did not yet exist, letters were folded so that none of the writing was visible. It was sealed with a glob of hot wax and the address was written on the outside. There were no street numbers, so the address usually mentioned a local landmark, such as "The 2nd house east of the Sign of the Sow tavern."

Another common and essential professional in colonial times was the miller. Custom millers existed mainly in small villages, where they ground grain for local farmers and kept some of the grain as their fee. In contrast, merchant millers lived and worked mainly in larger towns, where they bought grain in bulk from farmers, ground it into flour, and sold the flour far and wide. The grain was ground, or crushed, by large round stones called millstones, which turned by either wind or water power. (To take advantage of the power of moving water, many mills were built beside streams or waterfalls.)

No less important to colonists of all walks of life was the tanner, who cured animal hides and skins to make leather products. Leather, still popular today, was indispensable in a society in which no plastic or rubber yet existed. Some of the leather items common in colonial society included boots, shoes, pants, hats, aprons, harnesses for horses and other animals, carriage tops and curtains, buggy whips, and saddles. The leather-making process required considerable skill and involved a number of steps. Edwin Tunis, a noted authority on colonial life, explains:

> The tanner first prepared his hide. He split it down the middle into "sides" to make handling easier and trimmed away worthless ends.

Then he gave it a long soak in water to soften it. The hair could be loosened by further soaking in limewater, but small tanneries did this by simply stacking the wet hides for some days and letting them "sweat." Sweating was actually the beginning of rot, but it wasn't allowed to go far enough to hurt the leather. The hide was next thrown over a slanting "beam" and scraped with two-handled knives on the flesh side to take off not only the hair, but also the outer layer of skin.[41]

The tanner then washed the hide and treated it with tannic acid, derived from tree bark, which toughened and preserved it.

Other skilled professionals used the finished leather to make specific products. Cobblers made shoes, for instance, and hatters made hats, not only from leather, but from wool, felt, feathers,

Leather products, such as boots and saddles, were very important to the colonists. The tanner, shown here, prepares animal hides to make the leather products.

and other materials. Towns also had tailors to make coats, cloaks, capes, and other specialized clothes; bakers to bake bread and pastries; cutlers to make razors, saws, and other metal tools from iron or steel; joiners to construct chests, cabinets, tables, and other wooden furniture; silversmiths and coppersmiths to make various utensils, containers, and decorative items from silver and copper; wainwrights to make wagons and carts; housewrights to erect new homes and other buildings; and plumbers to craft lead products, including bullets, water pipes, urns, and statues (as opposed to modern plumbers, who install and repair water pipes and fixtures).

Crafts Dependent on Technology

Some other important colonial American crafts and occupations relied to a considerable degree on technology and how advanced it was at the time. Unfortunately for the colonies, the quality of the methods and products their craftsmen turned out depended on English craftsmen and authorities. The latter wanted to control technologies for their own benefit, shortchanging the colonists in the process.

A prominent example was the blacksmith trade. American blacksmiths made horseshoes, ox shoes, metal hinges, farm tools, nails, ax heads, and several other small-scale items from pig iron (an impure, somewhat brittle form of iron), but most of the iron mined in the colo-

nies was shipped back to England for use in that nation's ironworks. The mother country even passed a law that limited the amount of iron products the colonists could make for themselves so that England could maintain control of the lucrative iron-making process and the revenue it produced.

Meanwhile, American blacksmiths, whose knowledge and equipment were less advanced, continued to employ older, traditional methods. These included the use of charcoal (produced by burning wood) to heat the metal. "The colonial blacksmith blew his fire [thereby making it hotter] with an enormous bellows," Tunis explains. "It was the job of an apprentice to pump the bellows and keep the fire hot."[42] When the iron became soft, the blacksmith hammered it into various desired shapes. Only later, after the American Revolution, did American blacksmiths begin to import more advanced ironwork technologies from England, then the world's leader in industrial technology.

In a similar manner, the mother country tried at first to control the shipbuilding industry, which employed master craftsmen called shipwrights. (Larger ships required the services of many other specialized workers as well, including rope makers, sail makers, carpenters, and ironworkers.) By the 1600s, England had depleted most of its native forests. But there were healthy trees by the millions in the colonies. And at first English authorities laid claim to the best wood for use in the mother country. It

Early American Potters

Colonial Americans used pottery objects, such as bowls, cups, jars, and other containers, much more extensively than people do today. So nearly every village had at least one professional potter. (The earliest known American potter was Philip Drinker, who worked in Massachusetts in the 1630s.) Early American pottery was almost all redware, made from plain black clay that when baked had a reddish hue due to traces of iron oxide. The potter dug up the clay, sifted it with an iron sieve to remove pebbles and twigs, and cleaned it with water. Then he mixed in sand to add strength. He either pressed moistened clay into a plaster or metal mold or molded it with his hands on his potter's wheel, depending on the item he wanted to make. Then he baked the form he created in a kiln heated by a wood fire for up to twenty-five hours. Finally he glazed the hardened item with paint made from red or white lead. To make a green glaze, he added copper oxide. (Unfortunately, lead is poisonous; so lead poisoning was common among potters. Today, paint is no longer made with lead.)

was a long, expensive trip across the ocean, however, so many English ships came to be built in the colonies, creating an industry that employed thousands of colonists. This situation also allowed American shipwrights to keep up with the latest advances in naval technology.

The Rise of Science

Advances in technology went hand in hand with the rise of modern science, which closely coincided with the age of exploration and early settlement of North America. From the beginning, many settlers had a strong interest in natural science. "Curiosity about the flora and fauna of America was keen," according to Louis B. Wright, who also says,

> the mineralogy, botany, zoology, anthropology, and climatology of America were themes that excited the interests of explorers and settlers, as well as stay-at-home Europeans. The earliest manifestation of scientific investigation in the New World quite logically centered upon natural history.[43]

European interest in North America's natural history was so intense that one of the biggest selling books about the Americas in the late 1500s and early

Benjamin Franklin, pictured with his son William, is one of the most famous American scientists to emerge from the colonial era.

1600s was *Joyful News Out of the New Found World Wherein Is Declared the Rare and Singular Virtues of Diverse and Sundry Herbs, Trees, Oils, Plants, and Stones, with Their Applications, as well as for Physic as Chirugery, the Said Being Well Applied Bringeth Such Present Remedy for All Diseases, as May Seem Altogether Incredible.* Coinciding with this interest was the first experimental scientist in British America. Arriving in Jamestown in 1610, the year after it was first settled, Lawrence Bohun collected and tested plant specimens and various minerals.

More organized scientific studies arose farther north in Massachusetts when Harvard College was established in 1636. Its courses in botany, geometry, physics, and astronomy paved the way for later serious studies of these subjects by intellectual and inquisitive colonists. At least twenty-five colonial Americans became members of England's prestigious scientific organization, the Royal Society. They regularly sent scientific information and specimens back to eager English and other European researchers throughout the colonial period.

One of the leading colonial researchers was John Winthrop IV, who began teaching at Harvard in 1738. He championed the discoveries of Isaac Newton, an English physicist and mathematician who was also the president of the Royal Society from 1703 to 1727. Winthrop was the first to teach Newton's calculus in America. He also received shipment of and operated a telescope that had belonged to the great English astronomer Edmond Halley.

The self-taught Benjamin Franklin proved to be a leading American scientist as well. He was one of the first people on either side of the Atlantic to study the phenomenon of electricity. Researchers had observed static electricity for centuries. But no one knew if lighting was also a form of electricity until Franklin demonstrated it in 1752. In a now-famous experiment, he attached a piece of metal to a kite during a thunderstorm and managed to attract sparks of lightning. This earned him worldwide fame and led to the use of lightning rods to protect houses and barns from lightning strikes. Thanks to Winthrop, Franklin, and others like them, by the close of the colonial period the occupation of scientist had been added to the list that included farmer, cooper, blacksmith, and shipwright in a rapidly expanding new nation called the United States.

Chapter Five

Justice, Crime, and Punishment

Among the most pressing problems in all of the colonies of British America were crime and what to do with lawbreakers. The mother country had an old and fairly complex system of justice, with many laws on the books, along with traditional punishments for various crimes. For the most part, however, the early North American colonists had to start from scratch in this area. They did borrow several legal ideas and punishments from English society. But for a long time they did so in a piecemeal, inefficient way. In part this was because most early colonists believed that they were hardworking, God-fearing folk who were frankly more moral and upstanding than most people back in the mother country. And at first there was a naive belief in the colonies that very little crime would occur there; therefore an extensive legal system was unnecessary.

Over time, however, the reality set in that colonial society had just as many lawbreakers as other societies did. So new laws and punishments were adopted as local governments saw fit. But with no overall systematic approach to justice, including no professional police forces, law enforcement remained weak and insufficient in most towns and cities.

Moreover, justice was almost nonexistent in the frontier areas. In the backcountry of North Carolina and South Carolina, for example, huge gangs of criminals ran amok for decades, killing and pillaging at will. As scholar John C. Miller points out:

Neither the courts nor the justices of the peace were backed by sufficient authority to suppress the [lawbreakers]. It was not until law-abiding citizens took matters into their own hands and organized . . . bodies of armed men who tracked down the gangs and administered a rough and ready justice . . . that order was restored.[44]

In most places and times in colonial America, however, this sort of vigilante justice was rare. And overall, law-abiding colonists were forced to endure a level of crime and social disorder that would horrify and outrage modern Americans.

Courts and Justice

The inefficiency of colonial justice can be readily seen in the manner in which local authorities approached law enforcement and trying accused offenders in court. Because there were no paid police, enforcing the law fell on a handful of sheriffs and justices of the peace. In many colonies a single sheriff was charged with overseeing an entire county. Furthermore, going after lawbreakers was only one of many duties he performed. It was common, for instance, for the sheriff to also be the local tax collector and to oversee legal business among farmers, merchants, and traders.

Also, early sheriffs did not receive regular salaries; rather, a sheriff was most often paid small fees for performing individual tasks. If he could make the

Members of a family barricade themselves in their home against an attack by a band of criminals. Law enforcement was weak in the early decades of the colonial era. No professional police forces existed.

In colonial times the criminal justice system was guided more by religious beliefs than by legal facts. Most trials were heavily weighted against the accused person in an effort to get him or her to confess to the crime.

same amount of money for collecting a tax as he could for capturing a criminal, he naturally preferred the former because it was easier and less dangerous. Under these conditions, sheriffs were often too busy or lacked the motivation to deal with all the criminals.

The courts were also plagued by disorganization and lack of professionalism. Judges were not highly trained scholars and legal experts, as they are today. The average colonial judge was a political or religious leader chosen because he could read and write and was trusted in the community. Also, most judges, like the legal system itself, were guided less by the legal concepts of facts and fairness and more by religious considerations. The primary goal for a judge was to enforce God's will. This usually entailed having the accused person confess his or her guilt and to repent, hopefully in public court. A trial was not primarily designed to prove someone's guilt or innocence, therefore, but rather to provide a venue for satisfying God through the process of confession.

Indeed, most trials were heavily weighted against the accused person, or defendant. There was a district attorney–like official appointed by the colonial governor; his job was to vigorously prosecute the defendant and get him to confess. In contrast, defense attorneys were rarely seen in court. This was partly because few such lawyers existed in the colonies, but also because they were expensive, so only upper-class people could afford to hire them. (There were no court-appointed lawyers as in modern courts.) Thus, the vast majority of colonists accused of a crime had to defend themselves in court, and because they knew practically nothing about the law, they usually lost.

Colonial Jails

Defendants who lost their cases and were convicted did not usually go to prison, as is the most common criminal penalty meted out today. This was partly because serving a prison term takes time, sometimes many years, and requires housing, feeding, and clothing the convicts at public expense. A majority of colonists preferred quicker, less expensive punishments. Also, the populations of the colonies were small,

Crime Only Seemed Bad

When it became clear that the early New England colonies regularly experienced crime like other societies, concerned local leaders searched for explanations. One came from the governor of Plymouth Colony, William Bradford. In his book Of Plymouth Plantation, *he claims that crime only seemed bad in his colony because there were fewer people in Plymouth than in the mother country and because crimes were more easily noticed and prosecuted in the colony. Bradford writes:*

[C]rimes] are here more discovered and seen and made public by due search, inquisition, and due punishment. For the churches look narrowly to their members [and] more strictly than in other places. Besides, here the people are but few in comparison of other places, which are full and populous and [where crimes often] lie hidden, as it were, in a wood or thicket and many horrible evils . . . are never seen or known. Whereas [here crimes are] brought into the light [and] made conspicuous to the view of all.

William Bradford, *Of Plymouth Plantation*, ed. Samuel E. Morrison, New York: Knopf, 1959, pp. 316–17.

which meant that laborers of all kinds were always in demand. The general consensus of the citizenry was that locking people up for months or years reduced the labor force too much, another reason for speedier punishments.

The American colonies did have prisons, more accurately termed jails or cells because they were very small (usually consisting of only one or two rooms). But as a rule they were places where accused criminals awaited their trials, most often for a few days or weeks. These holding cells were dreary, uncomfortable, and unsanitary. "It occurred to no one in the eighteenth century," one expert observer writes:

> that a prison should have any quality other than strength. If you could keep a prisoner where you put him, his comfort and health needed no consideration. A colonial prison cell usually had one barred window, small and high. A bundle of straw was provided as a bed and the only thing in the way of a seat was [a crude, filthy toilet]. If a prisoner was at all aggressive, he was kept in irons. Food was passed to him through a slot.[45]

In fact, so little thought was given to inmates' comfort that if multiple prisoners were awaiting trial in the same town or county, they were all tossed into the same cell. A South Carolinian sent to jail in Charleston later called the experience barbaric, saying,

> Persons of every class [are] promiscuously [haphazardly] confined together in a space where they have not room to lie [down], and no distinction [is] made between offenders, but thieves and murderers, debtors to the king, offenders in penal laws, vagrants and idle persons are closely huddled in one mixed crowd.[46]

Public Humiliation

Because sending people to jail was not in the best interest of their communities, authorities generally relied on swifter, more dramatic punishments. These were viewed not only as retribution or justice for whatever crime had been committed, but also as deterrents, that is, ways to scare everyone in society into complying with the local laws. The belief was that suffering a certain punishment would deter a criminal from repeating his or her offense; it would also hopefully make noncriminals think twice about breaking the law. (Clearly, this approach failed miserably, as there was never a shortage of either repeat offenders or first-time criminals.)

Throughout the colonies the principal forms of punishment were public humiliation, physical maiming, and death. The obvious object of public humiliation was to embarrass the person so badly that he or she would learn a lesson and thereafter respect the law. One of the most common ways to humiliate someone was to put him or her in the

A physically uncomfortable and embarrassing punishment in colonial times was to place a person in a pillory.

stocks, which could be found in every colony in the 1600s. The stocks was a wooden apparatus in which a person sat, in public, with the legs extended forward and locked in place and immovable. One might remain in that position for a few hours or an entire day or more. Often people verbally abused the entrapped person or threw eggs or garbage at him or her.

In 1656 a Boston mariner named Kemble was placed in the stocks for two hours for the offense of kissing his wife in public after returning from a three-year sea journey. In another case, a Virginia man, Samuel Powell,

stole a pair of pants in 1638. His penalty was to "sit in the stocks on the next Sabbath day . . . from the beginning of morning prayer until the end of the Sermon with a pair of [pants hung] about his neck."[47]

Similar to the stocks was the pillory, sometimes called the "stretchneck." The difference was that the person stood on his or her feet, but bent over forward with the head and arms locked between pieces of wood. A wide range of offenses could send someone to the pillory, depending on the local laws. They included arson, perjury, blasphemy (verbally offending God),

Punishing Those with Idle Tongues

The brank, one common colonial punishment, might be classified as both a kind of humiliation and a means of inflicting pain and discomfort. It was also called the "gossip's bridle" or "scold's helm" because it was most often used on women who were seen to engage too much in gossip and idle talk. The device consisted of an iron cage that fit over the head. Projecting inward from the front rim was a flat piece of metal that was thrust into the person's mouth and pressed down hard on the tongue, preventing speech and often causing major physical and emotional distress. A less cumbersome tool for punishing gossips was the cleft stick. One cut a live twig from a tree or bush, split one end open, creating a cleft, and then forced the person's tongue into the cleft.

wife beating, slander, cheating at cards, fortune-telling (seen as antireligious), and drunkenness, to name only a few. One colonist spent a day in the pillory for playing a practical joke on someone. Others suffered this punishment because they were destitute and had resorted to begging for money. People often threw things at the person locked in the pillory. On occasion, the objects thrown caused serious injury or even death. This was seen as the offender's tough luck and no one was prosecuted for hurting or killing him or her.

Another humiliating form of punishment was the ducking stool, a chairlike seat attached to two wooden beams. The lawbreaker was tied to the seat and several men used the beams to swing it out over a pond or river, repeatedly forcing her or him under the water's surface. Scolds—women who gossiped too much—were the most common victims of this device. But sometimes a husband and wife whom neighbors felt fought too much were tied onto the seat back-to-back and dunked together.

One of the most dreaded humiliations of all in the eyes of most colonists was having to wear an emblem every day that advertised one's offense to the community. The emblem usually took the form of a printed sign worn around the neck or sewn onto one's shirt or dress. The sign most often bore a single letter that stood for the crime. A famous example is in Nathaniel Hawthorne's 1850 novel *The Scarlet Letter*, in which the colonial heroine, Hester Prynne, is forced to wear a bright red *A* on her dress for committing adultery. In addition, *B* stood for either burglar or blasphemer, *D* for drunkard, *F* for forger, *H* for hog stealer, *M* for manslaughter, and *T* for thief.

Physical Injury and Mutilation

Quite often a judge or a lawbreaker's neighbors felt that humiliation alone was not a strong enough penalty for him or her. In such cases the punishment chosen drew blood or maimed the person for life. A common example was permanently marking the offender with a let-

ter. Instead of wearing a sign bearing an *A*, *B*, *D*, or *T*, the offender was actually branded (using a red-hot iron) with the letter on his or her forehead.

Whipping was the most popular of these more severe punishments in most colonies (from the point of view of the spectators, who often gathered in large numbers to watch). Sometimes whipping

For very serious offenses, the accused was often tied to a post and whipped in the town square.

was applied to repeat offenders. In Pennsylvania in the 1700s, for instance, someone convicted of adultery three times in a row received twenty-one lashes (along with having the letter *A* branded on his or her forehead). But first-time offenders were frequently whipped as well. A German named Gottlieb Mittelberger who traveled to the colonies in 1750 later wrote:

If someone steals objects of as little value as a handkerchief, a pair of stockings, shoes, or a shirt, and suit is brought against him, he is tied to a post in the public market, stripped to the waist, and lashed so terribly with a switch or even with a horse- or dog-whip in which knots have sometimes been tied, that patches of skin and flesh hang down from his body.[48]

No less hideous and long-lasting scars were produced from other legally sanctioned mutilations. Sometimes when a person was condemned to the pillory, while his or her head was immobilized

"Witches" on Trial in Salem

Probably the most famous example of colonial justice is unfortunately also one of the most blatant miscarriages of justice in American history. The setting was Salem, Massachusetts, in 1692. Beginning with Elizabeth Parris and Abigail Williams, several young local girls started having strange and at times frightening fits. A number of adults in the community swiftly jumped to the conclusion that this unusual behavior was the result of witchcraft. In those days many people believed that witches were real. And witchcraft, demons, sorcery, and other supernatural elements were part of the accepted religious and social worldview of that era. Such pervasive ignorance and superstition brought about one of history's best-documented cases of mass hysteria.

The afflicted girls soon accused three women in the town of being witches. Since witchcraft was illegal in Salem, the accused women were put on trial. The trials soon spiraled out of control as neighbors and the authorities, gripped by fear, accused more and more people of being witches. Hundreds were sent to jail and twenty, including a minister and several frail elderly women, were executed, all members of the lower classes. Tellingly, however, when the young girls began accusing members of the upper class of being witches, the authorities, who belonged to that class, immediately ended the trials and called for reason.

someone hammered nails through the ears. In some cases, a common example being the offense of publicly insulting leading government officials, a person's ears were actually lopped off. And a number of religious heretics had holes drilled in their tongues by red-hot irons.

Death

The ultimate punishment, of course, was death. It was often inflicted for the second or third violation of almost any offense, even a minor one. Petty thieves were sometimes put to death for their second offense. And some people who stole neighbors' pigs three times in a row also went to the gallows. Many colonists thought the death penalty particularly fitting for sexual offenses and crimes against God.

And twenty people were executed in Salem, Massachusetts, in the 1690s after being convicted of practicing witchcraft. It took well over two centuries for American society to abandon such travesties of justice, to begin protecting the innocent as well as punishing the guilty, and, just as important, to make the punishment fit the crime.

Chapter Six

HEALTH, MEDICINE, AND DOCTORS

The English North American colonies were often a sort of crossroads of diseases from three continents. European settlers brought with them numerous kinds of germs. (Native Americans, of course, had no immunity to these ailments, which killed huge numbers of them.) Then the settlers were exposed to the germs of the Americas, as well as to African ones carried by the black slaves who were imported into the colonies in increasing numbers. Thus, according to scholar John C. Miller:

> A recently arrived European, however immunized to the diseases endemic in his native land, was obliged in America to withstand the onslaught of a disconcerting variety of germs, any one of which might prove fatal. Particularly if

he had been debilitated by illness and malnutrition, the usual consequence of a long sea voyage, he fell an easy prey to the host of microbes lying in wait for him.[49]

Many Debilitating Illnesses

Wherever the germs originated, they wiped out large numbers of colonists and Indians in the 1600s and 1700s. Common killers of one group or another in those days were measles, typhus, diphtheria, dysentery, malaria, yellow fever, cholera, scarlet fever, whooping cough, smallpox, and consumption (tuberculosis and other respiratory illnesses). And there were many others. English traveler John Josselyn, who visited New England in the mid-1600s, describes some of the ailments common in that region:

The stone [a kidney stone] terribly afflicts many, and the gout [pain in the joints and tendons], and sciatica [nerve pain]. Headaches are frequent, palsy [paralysis], dropsy [swelling of the tissues], worms . . . cancers, pestilent fevers, [and] scurvy [an illness caused by lack of vitamin C in the diet]. Also, they are troubled with a disease in the mouth or throat which has proved mortal [fatal] to some in a very short time.[50]

Historians sometimes find it hard to sort through the numerous colonial illnesses, as a number of those described in writings that survive from that era are now difficult to identify. This is partly because the names then used for them were generalized and imprecise. Lehmann College scholar David F. Hawke explains:

The flux, or bloody flux indicated some bowel disorder that could be anything from diarrhea to dysentery to typhoid fever. Cancer generally meant an ulcerous spreading sore. Consumption indicated a persistent respiratory illness that could vary from tuberculosis to pneumonia.

Many illnesses that affected the colonists were especially deadly to the Native American population, which had no immunity to diseases brought over from Europe.

No one then died of something that was specifically diagnosed as heart disease [though that ailment was surely common].[51]

Most of these illnesses were quite debilitating, both to individual families and entire communities and colonies. In a 1713 measles epidemic in Massachusetts, noted minister Cotton Mather lost five family members, including his wife. And terrible outbreaks of influenza (the flu), then called "malignant fever," swept through the colonies in 1732, 1760, and 1772. Even worse was a diphtheria epidemic that erupted in 1735. Within two years it had killed more than five thousand people in the New England colonies alone.

Other sicknesses, though not fatal, could be both uncomfortable and unsightly. Dental problems, for example, were common. Describing the ravages of tooth decay in the colonies, Josselyn writes, "The women are pitifully tooth-shaken. Whether [it is caused by] the coldness of the climate, or by [eating too many] sweet[s], I am not able to affirm."[52]

Folk Remedies and Cures

With a few exceptions, treatments for the various colonial diseases and medi-

Franklin Supports Inoculation

One of the most destructive diseases of the colonial era was smallpox, which struck British America repeatedly, killing thousands. Noted colonist Benjamin Franklin describes below a particularly bad outbreak that occurred in Boston from 1753 to 1754 and how inoculation helped reduce the death toll.

It had not spread in the town for many years before, so that there were a great number of the inhabitants to have it [because they had no immunity to it]. At first endeavors were used to prevent its spreading by removing the sick or guard-ing the houses in which they were, and with the same view inoculation was forbidden. But when it was found that these endeavors were fruitless [and the disease was spreading], inoculation was then permitted. Upon this, all [people who] inclined to inoculation for themselves or families hurried into it. . . . In a few months the distemper went through the town and was extinct. And the trade of the town suffered only a short interruption, compared with what had been usual in former times.

Benjamin Franklin, "A Collection of Letters," in *Collections of the Massachusetts Historical Society*, vol. 8, Boston: Massachusetts Hist orical Society, 1833, pp. 72–73.

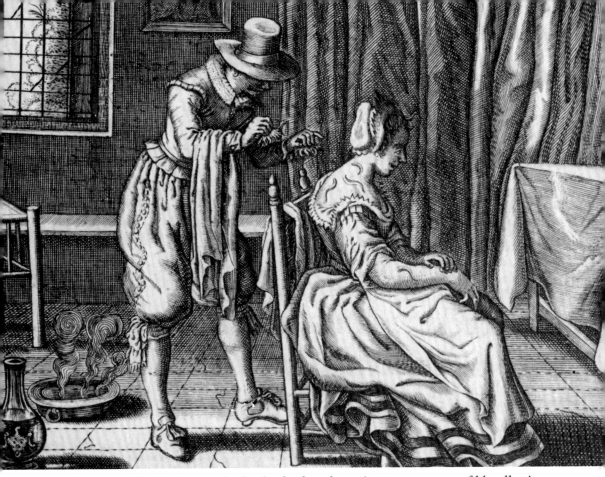

A doctor applies leeches to the back of a female patient as a means of bloodletting. At the time it was thought that bloodletting could cure almost any illness.

cal conditions were fairly ineffective. In part, this was because the causes of such illnesses, including germs, were still unknown. (The germ theory of disease was not introduced until the nineteenth century.) So quite frequently doctors and other healers fell back on traditional folk remedies, a number of them holdovers from ancient and medieval times.

A majority of the available "medicines" were either worthless or actually made the patient's condition worse. Patients would eat kidney beans to strengthen the kidneys or treat kidney ailments, snake balls (snake parts mixed with chalk) to relieve stomach pain, and snake oil (snake fat) to cure gout. Another common remedy that had no medicinal effect was using sassafras root to treat syphilis (a serious sexually transmitted disease). Other silly folk remedies included trying to cure toothaches with a mixture of flour, milk, corn, and hog fat; dropping hedgehog fat into the ear to cure deafness; stopping a headache with a combination of blood from a male cat and human breast milk; carrying around a horse chestnut in hopes of warding off rheumatism (arthritis and other joint diseases); and consuming rattlesnake root (an extremely bitter-tasting plant) supposedly to combat most known diseases. These "cures" illustrate, among other things, a common belief of that era. Namely, the more bizarre and/or disgusting a medicine was, the better the chance it would drive away illness.

Among the purported treatments that only ended up hurting patients was tobacco. Virginia's wealthy planter William Byrd promoted it as a remedy (likely because he grew tobacco and the more that people used it the richer he became). During his travels, Josselyn wrote, "The virtues of tobacco are these: it helps digestion, the gout, the tooth-ache . . . purges the stomach, kills nits and lice, [and cures] all diseases of a cold and moist cause."[53] It is notable that this ludicrous notion of tobacco as a medicine was perpetuated well into the twentieth century in some places before medical science finally proved beyond doubt that it kills hundreds of thousands of Americans each year.

There were also some common medical procedures that hurt rather than helped patients. Perhaps the most prevalent of these was phlebotomy, better known as bleeding or bloodletting. According to one writer:

doctors bled patients for every ailment imaginable. They bled for pneumonia and fevers, back pain and rheumatism, headaches and melancholia; even to treat bone fractures and other wounds. Yet there never was any evidence that phlebotomy did any good. Bloodletting was based on an ancient system of medicine in which blood and other bodily fluid were considered to be "humors" whose proper balance maintained health. Sick patients were thought to have an imbalance of their humors, which bloodletting was thought to restore. Most bloodletters would open a vein in the arm, leg or neck with [a] small, fine knife called a lancet. They would tie off the area with a tourniquet and, holding the lancet delicately between thumb and forefinger, strike diagonally or lengthwise into the vein. [Finally] they would collect the blood in measuring bowls.[54]

Despite this litany of useless remedies and treatments, some herbs and other home remedies were effective. It was found, for instance, that quinine, a bitter liquid made from a certain kind of tree bark, helped to reduce the symptoms of malaria. And some people promoted the use of ginseng root, which evidence suggests can help alleviate stress. Among those who swore by ginseng was William Byrd, who wrote:

To help cure fatigue, I used to chew a root of ginseng as I walked along. This kept up my spirits. It gives an uncommon warmth and vigor to the blood. It cheers the heart of a

Sickness Caused by Bad Conduct?

People in colonial times had numerous mis-conceptions about disease and why people got sick. Not knowing that germs cause disease, they typically blamed illnesses on unrelated factors, such as climate or personal misconduct. A man from South Carolina in the mid-1700s explains:

If people are sick [in the Carolinas] 'tis generally an effect of their bad conduct and not knowing how to regulate themselves suitably to the country where they live. For 'tis very certain that those who observe precautions have as good health there as they would in other places. But the better to understand this affair, you must know that the uncultivated lands of Carolina [are] very cold in their nature, and when the vapors which they have attracted and retained come to be dispersed by a northerly wind, you feel a cold almost as sharp as in Europe.... This then, together with [drinking and eating too much] is the real source of the sicknesses there.

Jean Pierre Purry, *A Description of the Province of South Carolina*, Washington, DC: U.S. Government Printing Office, 1837, p. 10.

man that has a bad wife, and makes him look down with great composure upon the crosses of the world. It will make old age amiable by rendering it lively, cheerful, and good humored.[55]

Colonial Doctors

In theory, any colonist could bleed or administer herbs and medicines to a sick person. But most often it was a physician of some kind who did so. In the early 1600s, when North America was first being settled, there were three basic kinds of doctor in England and other parts of Europe. One was a university graduate (or an apprentice of a graduate) with some understanding of medical history and theory; another was the "surgeon" (often a barber), who performed various operations for a fee; the third was the apothecary (now called a pharmacist), who made and sold drugs and medicines. In the colonies, it became clear over time that there were not enough patients to support all three professions. So they more or less merged into one. By the end of the 1600s, "the American doctor served as physician to his patients, did his own surgery, and concocted his own drugs,"[56] writes Hawke.

Yet only a minority of such doctors was highly skilled and reliable. "Few physicians among us are eminent for their skill," complained a colonial New Yorker

In the 1700s the medical profession slowly became more formal and regulated. Dr. Benjamin Rush, pictured, was one of the first university-trained doctors to come out of the colonies.

in 1757. "Quacks abound like locusts in Egypt, and too many have recommended themselves to a full and profitable practice and subsistence. This is the less to be wondered at, as the profession is under no kind of regulation."[57] One of the few reliable physicians, Alexander Hamilton (no relation to the famous patriot of that name), stated that he knew a doctor who had begun his career selling turnips on street corners. Also, in some cases ministers were called on to heal the sick. This was because it was widely believed that they were closer to God than average people were. Furthermore, whatever their backgrounds, most doctors had the reputation of charging too much for their services. The Virginia legislature alone passed four different laws regulating what doctors could charge.

Nevertheless, the quality of physicians did slowly improve over time. Following a number of skilled, dedicated doctors in the early 1700s, the first great medical researcher and physician in the colonies was Pennsylvania's Benjamin Rush (1745–1813). In later life, he described why he had become a doctor and how he had devoted much of his time to treating the less fortunate. He recalled,

My natural disposition made [being a doctor] very agreeable to me, for I had a natural sympathy with distress of every kind. My conduct during my appreticeship moreover paved the way for my success [because] I made myself acceptable at that time to the poor by my services to them [and] I began business among them. . . . My shop was crowded with the poor in the morning and at meal times. . . . There are very few old huts now standing in [Philadelphia, Pennsylvania] in which I have not attended sick people. . . . I review these scenes with heartfelt pleasure, [and] to [God's] goodness in accepting my services to His poor children, I ascribe [credit] the innumerable blessings of my life.[58]

Governor Winthrop's Home Remedies

Noted American physician and professor Oliver Wendell Holmes Sr. (1809–1894) was fascinated by colonial medicines and cures and wrote a long essay on the subject. It includes the following passage about the medical dabbling of the early Massachusetts governor John Winthrop.

His great remedy, which he gave oftener than any other, was nitre [potassium nitrate, or saltpeter], which he ordered in doses of twenty or thirty grains to adults, and of three grains to infants. Measles, colic, sciatica, headache, giddiness, and many other ailments, all found themselves treated, and I trust bettered, by nitre, a pretty safe medicine in moderate doses, and one not likely to keep the good governor awake at night, thinking whether it might not kill, if it did not cure. We may say as much for spermaceti [an extract of sperm oil from whales], which he seems to have considered [the best cure] for inward bruises, and often prescribes after falls and similar injuries. One of the next remedies, in point of frequency, which he was in the habit of giving, was . . . antimony, a mild form of that very active metal, and which, mild as it was, left his patients very commonly with a pretty strong conviction that they had been taking something that did not exactly agree with them.

Oliver Wendell Holmes, *Medical Essays*, Boston: Boston Society for the Diffusion of Useful Knowledge, 1842. Also available at http://chestofbooks .com/health/general/Oliver-Wendell-Holmes-Medical-Essays/The-Medical-Profession-In-Massachusetts-Part-5.html.

Colonial Medical Advances

Thanks to men like Rush, colonial medicine made several advances, especially in the second half of the eighteenth century. Clergyman-doctors steadily disappeared. Also, although there was still no known connection between germs and disease, quarantining the sick became more common. In addition, some doctors began to practice in more sanitary conditions.

The medical practice of inoculation was introduced in the mid-1700s. When used in the fight against smallpox, inoculation was a success; but the procedure was banned in many colonies for years due to lack of knowledge about it.

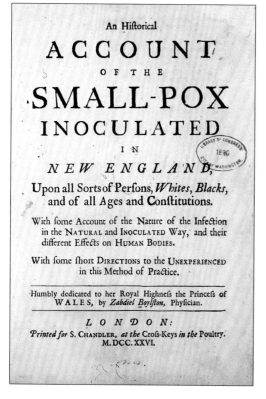

An Historical

ACCOUNT

OF THE

·SMALL-POX

INOCULATED

IN

NEW ENGLAND,

Upon all Sorts of Perfons, *Whites, Blacks,* and of all Ages and Conftitutions.

With fome Account of the Nature of the Infection in the NATURAL and INOCULATED Way, and their different Effects on HUMAN BODIES.

With fome fhort DIRECTIONS to the UNEXPERIENCED in this Method of Practice.

Humbly dedicated to her Royal Highnefs the Princefs of WALES, by *Zabdiel Boylſton,* Phyſician.

LONDON:

Printed for S. CHANDLER, *at the* Crofs-Keys *in the* Poultry. M.DCC.XXVI.

Particularly important was an increase in the number of university-trained physicians like Rush. The first modern hospital in North America opened in Philadelphia in 1755. And several of its doctors created the first colonial medical school, at that city's college (later the University of Pennsylvania), in 1765. Three years later, King's College (later Columbia University) in New York opened another reputable medical school.

Another important medical advance was the practice of inoculation, in which a healer deliberately infects a person with a form of a disease to prevent future illness in that person. (Someone who is inoculated builds up a tolerance for the illness.) Inoculation, which had been introduced earlier in Europe and Africa, first took hold in the colonies in 1721. During the smallpox outbreak that struck Boston, Massachusetts, that year, Cotton Mather convinced a physician friend, Zabdiel Boylston, to attempt the then controversial treatment. Boylston first removed scabs from some of his smallpox patients. He ground them into a fine powder. Then he made cuts in the arms of some test subjects and sprinkled some of the powder in the cuts. This experiment proved a success, as the people Boylston had inoculated later seemed immune to smallpox. Mather then called for all Bostonians to be inoculated, but too many people remained afraid of the procedure (thinking it would cause rather than cure smallpox) and local leaders banned its use.

The heroic Boylston continued inoculating patients in secret, however. And fearing that his son, Samuel, might catch smallpox, Mather had the doctor inoculate the young man, who survived with no ill effects. Unfortunately, fear of the disease was so great that when some locals found out, they tossed a bomb through Mather's window in the middle of the night. Thankfully no one was injured.

Despite these protests against inoculation, the treatment became increasingly common both in Europe and the American colonies. Benjamin Franklin was among several prominent colonists who advocated it. It did remain illegal in many of the colonies for a few decades, but these bans were later lifted, and during the American Revolution, George Washington had all of his soldiers inoculated. This event alone was a testament to the rise of colonial American medical science. It had begun under a pall of ignorance and superstition. But through the hard work, courage, and dedication of a few, it became far more reputable and reliable.

Chapter Seven

LEISURE, RECREATION, AND SPORTS

Like people everywhere throughout history, colonial Americans sometimes sought ways to relax and enjoy themselves. But the degree to and manner in which they did so was affected by three overriding factors. First, in the early 1600s, when English and other European groups were initially settling the colonies, they were engaged in a nearly relentless struggle for survival. So there was precious little time for leisure activities. Only when basic needs such as housing, food supplies, and security were firmly in place could the colonists allow themselves the luxury of downtime and recreation on a regular basis. Second, some groups of settlers, notably the Puritans, actually rejected the idea of recreation and having fun. And it took a few generations for them to allow their natural tendency for play to find personal and social expression.

Finally, the ways in which the colonists had fun were largely determined by the social and technological realities of their day. Most of them were English. And it was only natural that they would seek to entertain themselves as people in England had for generations. Also, the technical advances that make today's widespread mechanical and electronic forms of entertainment possible were still far in the future. So people had to be creative in devising ways to enjoy themselves. According to Louis B. Wright:

colonial people, wherever they lived, had fewer amusements that they could buy than even the most deprived person has today. No moving picture [movie], no radio, no television, no comic strip, no cheap paperback book, no amusement park, no automobile, no social service to organize entertainment, no belief anywhere that something must be done to help people utilize their leisure. Such entertainment as people had, young or old, they had to devise for themselves. Their amusements came from participation, not from looking on. Spectator sports, except for horse racing, cockfighting, and few similar activities, were almost nonexistent. To find enjoyment, one had to take part in something. This necessarily trained our ancestors to develop their own inner resources.[59]

Fun Frowned Upon

The Puritans, who created Massachusetts Bay and other New England colonies, certainly possessed strong inner resources. But they had learned to channel them almost exclusively toward religious devotion and personal and social discipline. And they did this to an extent that most people today would see as bizarre. Puritanism of that era imposed "a code of daily life and a set of values that strained human character to its limits," one historian explains. "At the heart of the Puritan faith was the notion that all people since Adam's fall were depraved and deserved damnation." So people were expected to behave well and "avoid wicked thoughts and feelings."[60] Under such conditions, the concepts of play and fun were generally frowned upon.

It was not just games and leisure activities that were discouraged, however. Most social and religious celebrations taken for granted today were also condemned. In 1644 the Puritans actually banned Christmas. Calling it wasteful and dangerous to true Christian faith, they tried to suppress all Christmas customs, from mince pies to decorating with holly.

The Puritan prohibitions against fun, recreation, and relaxation were particularly strict on Sunday, the so-called Sabbath or Lord's Day. On that day in the 1600s, no labor could be performed in most of New England. This included cooking, cleaning, or even making beds. No travel or other sort of recreation was allowed either, a ban that extended even to going for a walk in the countryside. In 1670 in New London, Connecticut, two young people, John Lewis and Sarah Chapman, were tried in court for "sitting together on the Lord's Day under an apple tree in Goodman Chapman's orchard." And in Plymouth, Massachusetts, in 1652, housewife Elizabeth Eddy was fined "ten shillings for wringing and hanging out clothes" on Sunday.[61]

Most English travelers who visited New England in that era were astounded at how strict the Sabbath laws were in the region. In the 1730s one such traveler, Joseph Bennett, wrote:

> On that day, no man, woman, or child is permitted to go out of town on any pretense whatsoever, nor can any that are out of town come in on the Lord's Day. [And] as they

will by no means admit of trading [shopping or business] on Sundays, so they are equally tenacious [stubborn] about preserving order . . . on the Lord's Day. And they will not suffer anyone to walk down to the waterside . . . nor even in the hottest days of summer will they admit of anyone to take the air [in the town square].[62]

A young Puritan woman reads as she spins yarn. The Puritans possessed a strong religious devotion and personal and social discipline.

Strictly Observing the Sabbath

The Puritans who established Boston, Massachusetts, in the early 1600s were extremely austere and severe about personal conduct and looked down on playing and various forms of amusement. Some of that attitude carried over into the early 1700s. English traveler John Bennett visited Boston in the 1730s and viewed what he thought to be overly strict bans on normal activities on Sundays. Bennett writes:

If two or three people, who meet one another in the street by accident, stand talking together . . . they are liable to fine and imprisonment. And I believe, whos-ever incurs the penalties on this account, are sure to feel the weight of them. But that which is the most extraordinary is, that they commence the Sabbath from the setting of the sun on the Saturday evening. And in conformity to that, all trade and business ceases, and every shop in the town is shut up. Even a barber is fined for shaving [someone] after that time. Nor are any of the taverns permitted to entertain company, for in that case, not only the house, but every person found therein is fined.

Joseph Bennett, *History of New England*, Boston: Massachusetts Historical Society, 1862, p. 116.

Upper-Class Pastimes

Over time, however, such restrictions began to ease. And in any case, people in several of the colonies engaged in all manner of amusements and leisure activities on weekdays. This was particularly true from the late 1600s on, by which time colonial societies had become well established and featured a certain amount of leisure time each week or month.

To some degree, the choice of such activities depended on one's wealth and social rank. Well-to-do planters, especially in the southern colonies, enjoyed fancy dinner dances, for example, to which poorer folk were not invited. Then often called "assemblies," and later "balls," they were held in mansions or large rooms in respectable inns and featured small orchestras. In addition to slow, stately dances, like the minuet, the guests let loose with all manner of faster, more energetic ones. Among these were contra dances (later called square dances), the lively Virginia reel, and various informal jigs. No matter how informal the dances, however, dress remained quite formal; ladies wore huge hoop skirts and men donned powdered wigs and lace-covered jackets.

Such gatherings were often long, spirited, and sometimes even broke some social rules. According to Wright:

young planters would ride for miles to attend these assemblies and would dance all night to music supplied sometimes by trained musicians, but more often by white indentured servants whose skills had been discovered and developed, or, late in the period, by Negro fiddlers who had learned the art from white musicians. So fond of dancing were the Virginians that they sometimes danced the whole night through and into the next day. On one occasion, late in the seventeenth century, the daughter of Reverend Thomas Teakle, a well-to-do minister of Accomac County, created a scandal by giving a dance on a Saturday night while her father was absent from home. The company, carried away with enthusiasm, danced until the very hour of church service the next day, which [both the minister and community frowned on].[63]

The ability to dance was so important to upper-class folk in Virginia, Maryland, and the Carolinas that dancing teachers and schools came into fashion in those colonies in the early 1700s. In 1716 officials at the College of William and Mary allowed a dancing instructor named William Levingstone to hold dancing classes in a room on campus. Such classes eventually became a regu-

Fond Memories of Dancing

In 1773 Philip Fithian, a young minister who tutored the children of a wealthy Virginia planter, attended a party. During the party, a dancing teacher named Mr. Christian impressed the guests with his ability to do the minuet, after which everyone joined in various popular dances. Fithian recalls:

[I saw] several Minuets danced with great ease and propriety [politeness], after which the whole company joined in country-dances [square dances] and it was indeed beautiful to admiration to see such a number of young persons, set off by dress to the best advantage [well dressed], moving easily to the sound of well-performed music and with perfect regularity. . . . When it was too dark to dance, the young gentlemen walked over to my room. We conversed till half after six [six thirty].

Quoted inWorld Book, *Christmas in Colonial and Early America*, Chicago: World Book, 1996, pp. 12–13.

By the early 1700s, leisure time was a more accepted part of society. Here, party goers dance the minuet at a fancy dinner-dance.

lar feature at the college. And there were also many itinerant dancing teachers who traveled around the colonies holding seminars for anyone with the money and time.

Well-to-do southerners also greatly enjoyed horse racing. Many rich planters owned extensive riding stables and entered their horses in various local contests. Betting on potential winners was frequently heavy, as gambling was a common leisure pastime in the region. Horse races were held in some northern colonies as well, particularly in Rhode Island, which had a number of planta-

tions similar to those in the South. In fact, for a while Rhode Island was the leading horse-breeding area in the colonies. According to an expert on colonial American horses:

Rhode Island's horse industry got its beginning when John Hull, treasurer of the Massachusetts Bay Colony, purchased land on the west side of [Rhode Island's] Narragansett Bay from the local Indians. This area was fenced off and set up for horse breeding. At one time Rhode Island had farms with as many as

Travelers' Inns

One diversion from everyday life in colonial times was traveling to other towns and colonies. But lacking airplanes, trains, and cars, these journeys took much longer than they do now. A trip from New York to Boston could then take up to three days, for instance. So inns to accommodate travelers along the way became necessary. They were located mainly at crossroads, ferries, and in towns. Most had simply adequate beds and food. But a few were more luxurious and the finest of all—the Sun in Bethle-hem, Pennsylvania—even provided servants for well-to-do customers.

One modern scholar calls these inns combination diners and tourist houses because they provided both food and leisure activities in addition to beds for the night. One could go to an inn just to have a drink (rum and ale were always popular). Or a person could get together with other people there for political discussions, catching up on the latest news, playing cards and other forms of gambling, or playing checkers (then called draughts).

1,000 horses, predominantly Narragansett Pacers. From these Rhode Island farms, horses were shipped to all of the sea-coast colonies, as well as to the islands of the Caribbean. . . . Rhode Island was the only New England colony which allowed horse racing, and a one-mile track was maintained at Sandy Neck Beach, South Kingston.[64]

More Earthy Pastimes

It should be noted that people of lower social rank sometimes held less-formal horse races of their own, even in colonies where the sport was unlawful. And there were numerous other, more earthy pastimes enjoyed by the masses. Hunting and fishing, for example, were widely popular in all the colonies and among all classes. In part this was because these activities were open and free to all, with no hunting or fishing licenses required. Men were apt to go after any forest creature with either guns or traps, but deer, foxes, and wolves were particular favorites. Most young boys were fond of hunting rabbits.

Meanwhile, fish of many varieties were available not only at the seashore, but also in inland lakes, rivers, and streams. Fishing enthusiasts employed both the hook and line and nets, depending on the situation. Hunting and fishing had an added dimension in colonial days: Besides being recreational activities, they provided food for the table.

Another popular colonial pastime that is now illegal is cockfighting. Both rich and poor people bred their own gamecocks (roosters trained for fighting) and staged fights for neighbors or the public, providing another major outlet for betting money and other valuables. The creatures were trained to kill their opponents. And it was common for owners to attach steel spurs to their feet to make their blows more deadly. Some owners also tried to cheat, either by putting garlic on a bird's beak to ward off its opponent or giving the animal a shot of brandy to make it more fearless.

Also cruel and barbaric was the so-called sport of bullbaiting. Brought to the colonies from England, where it was popular in late medieval times, it consisted of people watching dogs attack a bull. One such event was held in Pennsylvania in the 1700s. That particular occasion turned out to be highly unusual due to the sudden intervention of someone who felt bad for the bull. An observer at the time recalls:

The animal [the bull] was in a great rage, though much exhausted before I reached the scene of

A popular colonial pastime was fishing. This activity was enjoyable, yet also practical as the catch could feed a family at the end of the day.

action. Soon after I got there, the bull threw a small mastiff [a type of dog] about ten foot high, which [it] hooked in the upper jaw and tore it nearly off with every tooth in it. A new pack of dogs were now prepared for the combat, and every eye turned toward them. At this moment [a young woman named Polly Heffernan], pitying the persecuted animal, [ran] directly up to the bull, without [her] shoes or stockings on. . . . When she reached the bull, which almost immediately before was in a great rage, he dropped his ears, and [as he bowed his] head . . . she thus [said to] him, "Poor bully! And have they hurt you? They shall not hurt you any more." . . . We [men] were confounded and dumbstruck with amazement. Not a man dared to enter the ring to save her, but all stood trembling for Polly's life. [But then she ran away] and here the [bull] bait ended.[65]

Much more common, not to mention humane, was sleigh riding, which was especially popular in the mid-Atlantic and northern colonies where winters were longer and produced more snow. In her diary, a New York woman named Sarah Knight described sleigh rides in that colony in 1704, in which the riders afterward enjoyed lavish dinner parties. Knight wrote:

Their diversions in the winter [are] riding sleighs about three or four miles out of town, where they have houses of entertainment at a place called the Bowery, and some go to friends' houses. . . . [We went to the house of] one Madame Dowes, [who] gave us a handsome entertainment of five or six dishes and choice beer . . . all of which she said was the produce of her farm. I believe we met 50 or 60 sleighs that day. They fly with great swiftness and some are so furious that they'll turn out of the path for none except a loaded cart.[66]

Still another leisure diversion consisted of local fairs, held once or twice a year in several colonies. They were the ancestors of today's country and state fairs. People not only bought and sold a wide range of handmade foods, clothing, and other products, but also bartered cows, pigs, and other farm animals. They also staged all manner of contests. Among them were foot races; wrestling matches (as a young Virginian, George Washington was known for his wrestling skills); fights with cudgels (long sticks), like those described in the Robin Hood legends; and singing, dancing, and whistling competitions. Also popular at the fairs were puppet shows, rope-walking exhibitions, and fortune-tellers. Clearly colonial Americans had no trouble devising ways to amuse themselves.

Notes

Introduction: Islands in the Wilderness

1. James M. Volo and Dorothy D. Volo, *Daily Life on the Old Colonial Frontier*, Westport, CT: Greenwood, 2002, p. 2.
2. Quoted in Louis B. Wright, *The Atlantic Frontier: Colonial American Civilization, 1607–1763*, New York: Knopf, 1997, p. 124.
3. Volo and Volo, *Daily Life on the Old Colonial Frontier*, pp. 2–3.
4. David F. Hawke, *Everyday Life in Early America*, New York: Harper and Row, 1989, p. 20.
5. Hawke, *Everyday Life in Early America*, p. 31.
6. Louis B. Wright, *Everyday Life in Colonial America*, New York: Putnam's, 1965, p. 40.
7. Wright, *Everyday Life in Colonial America*, p. 56.
8. John C. Miller, *The First Frontier: Life in Colonial America*, Lanham, MD: University Press of America, 1986, p. 122.
9. Louis B. Wright, *The Cultural Life of the American Colonies, 1607–1763*, New York: Harper and Row, 2002, p. 1.

Chapter One: The Home and Its Contents

10. Wright, *Everyday Life in Colonial America*, pp. 214–15.
11. Miller, *First Frontier*, p. 175.
12. Jaspar Danckaerts, *The Journal of Jaspar Danckaerts, 1679–1680*, eds. Bartlett Burleigh James and J. Franklin Jameson, in *Original Narratives of Early American History*, ed. J. Franklin Jameson, New York: Barnes and Noble, 1941. Also available at www.archive.org/stream/journalofjasperd00danc/journalofjasperd00danc_djvu.txt.
13. Pehr Kalm, *Travels into North America*, vol. 2, trans. Adolph B. Benson, New York: Wilson-Erickson, 1937, p. 605.
14. Miller, *First Frontier*, p. 178.
15. Quoted in Frank R. Diffenderffer, *The German Immigration into Pennsylvania*, Lancaster: Pennsylvania German Society, 1900, p. 27.
16. Volo and Volo, *Daily Life on the Old Colonial Frontier*, p. 150.
17. Edwin Tunis, *Colonial Living*, Baltimore: Johns Hopkins University Press, 1999, p. 44.

Chapter 2: Women, Courtship, and Marriage

18. Benjamin Franklin, letter to Deborah Franklin, April 5, 1757, *Miscellaneous Benjamin Franklin Collections*, American Philosophical Society. Also available at www.familytales.org/dbDisplay.php?id=ltr_ben1523&person=ben.
19. Samuel Sewall, *The Diary of Samuel Sewall, 1674–1729*, vol. 2, ed. M. Halsey Thomas, New York: Farrar, Straus, and Giroux, 1973, p. 927.
20. John Winthrop, personal journal, April 13, 1634, www.constitution.org/primarysources/winthrop.html.
21. Elizabeth G. Speare, *Life in Colonial America*, New York: Random House, 1963, p. 69.
22. Charles W. Eliot, *American Contributions to Civilization*, New York: Century, 1897, p. 358.
23. Speare, *Life in Colonial America*, p. 73.
24. Volo and Volo, *Daily Life on the Old Colonial Frontier*, p. 25.
25. Quoted in William Kephart and Davor Jedlicka, *The Family, Society, and the Individual*, New York: HarperCollins, 1991, pp. 63–64.
26. Quoted in Arthur C. Calhoun, *A Social History of the American Family*, vol. 1, Cleveland, OH: Clark, 1917, p. 253.
27. Quoted in Harriott H. Ravenel, *Eliza Pinckney*, Whitefish, MT: Kessinger, 2007, pp. 55–56.
28. Volo and Volo, *Daily Life on the Old Colonial Frontier*, p. 121.
29. Miller, *First Frontier*, p. 200.

Chapter Three: Children and Education

30. Miller, *First Frontier*, p. 210.
31. Quoted in Speare, *Life in Colonial America*, p. 98.
32. Quoted in Alice M. Earle, *Child Life in Colonial Days*, Westminster, MD: Heritage, 2009, pp. 191–92.
33. Earle, *Child Life in Colonial Days*, p. 197.
34. Speare, *Life in Colonial America*, p. 102.
35. Quoted in Edmund Quincy, *Life of Josiah Quincy of Massachusetts*, Boston: Ticknor and Fields, 1867, p. 25.
36. Benjamin Franklin, *The Autobiography of Benjamin Franklin*, Reading, PA: Spencer, 1936, p. 13.
37. *New England's First Fruits*, New York: Sabin, 1865, pp. 23–24.
38. Quoted in James A. Williams, "Education in Massachusetts Bay," The Order of the Founders and Patriots of America (Web site), www.founderspatriots.org/articles/mass_education.htm.

Chapter Four: Occupations, Work, and Technology

39. Kalm, *Travels in North America*, pp. 307–308.
40. Franklin, *The Autobiography of Benjamin Franklin*, pp. 25–26.

41. Edwin Tunis, *Colonial Craftsmen and the Beginnings of American Industry,* Baltimore: Johns Hopkins University Press, 1999, pp. 22–23.

42. Tunis, *Colonial Living,* p. 57.

43. Wright, *The Cultural Life of the American Colonies,* p. 216.

Chapter Five: Justice, Crime, and Punishment

44. Miller, *First Frontier,* pp. 262–63.

45. Tunis, *Colonial Living,* p. 154.

46. Quoted in Merrill Jenson, ed., *American Colonial Documents to 1776,* New York: Oxford University Press, 1955, p. 595.

47. Quoted in James A. Cox, "Bilboes, Brands, Branks: Colonial Crimes and Punishments," Colonial Williamsburg Foundation, www.history.org/foundation/journal/Spring03/branks.cfm.

48. Gottlieb Mittelberger, Journey to Pennsylvania, eds. *Oscar Handlin and John Clive,* Cambridge, MA: Harvard University Press, 1960, p. 72.

Chapter Six: Health, Medicine, and Doctors

49. Miller, *First Frontier,* p. 237.

50. John Josselyn, *An Account of Two Voyages to New England,* Cambridge: Massachusetts Historical Society, 1833, pp. 331–34.

51. Hawke, *Everyday Life in Early America,* p. 81.

52. Josselyn, *An Account of Two Voyages to New England,* p. 334.

53. Josselyn, *An Account of Two Voyages to New England,* p. 262.

54. Douglas Starr, "Bloodletting," PBS, www.pbs.org/wnet/redgold/basics/bloodletting.html.

55. Quoted in Planet Botanic, "Ginseng," Planet Botanic, www.planetbotanic.ca/fact_sheets/ginseng_fs.htm.

56. Hawke, *Everyday Life in Early America,* p. 85.

57. Quoted in James H. Walsh, *History of Medicine in New York: Three Centuries of Medical Progress,* vol. 1, New York: National Americana Society, 1919, p. 75.

58. Benjamin Rush, *A Memorial Containing the Travels Through Life or Sundry Incidents in the Life of Dr. Benjamin Rush,* Philadelphia: Biddle, 1905, pp. 54–59.

Chapter Seven: Leisure, Recreation, and Sports

59. Wright, *Everyday Life in Colonial America,* pp. 212–13.

60. Irwin Unger, *These United States: The Questions of Our Past,* Boston: Little, Brown, 2002, pp. 51–52.

61. Quoted in Alice M. Earle, *Sabbath in Puritan New England,* Whitefish, MT: Kessinger, 2004, p. 146.

62. Joseph Bennett, *History of New England,* Boston: Massachusetts Historical Society, 1862, p. 115.

63. Wright, *Everyday Life in Colonial America,* pp. 180, 190.

64. International Museum of the Horse, "Return to the World: Colonial Horses," International Museum of the Horse, http://www.imh.org/history.php?chapter=56

65. Quoted in Hawke, *Everyday Life in Early America,* pp. 97–98.

66. Quoted in *Madam Knight, The Private Journal of a Journey from Boston to New York in the Year 1704,* Albany, NY: Little, 1865, pp. 70–71.

Glossary

apothecary: A person who made and sold drugs and medicines.

assembly: A dance or ball.

bleeding: An antiquated medical procedure in which large amounts of blood were drained from a patient; also known as bloodletting.

bullbaiting: A brutal exhibition in which dogs attack a bull.

bundling: An early colonial custom in which a boy and a girl lay together, fully clothed, in bed.

consumption: In colonial America, tuberculosis, pneumonia, or some other respiratory ailment.

cooper: A barrel maker.

crewelwork: Wool embroidery.

cudgel: A long stick used in stick-fighting contests.

dame school: Classes taught by a housewife in her home.

dowry: Money or valuables provided by a bride's parents for her maintenance during her marriage.

dropsy: In colonial America, a swelling of the bodily tissues.

dunking stool: A seatlike device in which a person who was being punished was tied and submerged in water.

groaning cakes: Food served to visitors during a woman's labor and childbirth.

hornbook: A text that school students copied to gain writing practice; also called a copybook.

inoculation: Using a form of a disease (such as scabs) to prevent future infections.

johnnycake: A flat bread made from cornmeal.

joiner: An early name for a carpenter, specifically one who made furniture.

keeping room: The main room in an early colonial house; also called the "hall."

minuet: A stately dance popular in Europe and America in the 1600s and 1700s.

old-friend schools: Classes taught by itinerant (traveling) teachers.

pillory: A wooden framework in which a person who was being punished stood with the head and arms locked in place.

plumber: In colonial America, a person who made bullets, water pipes, and other products from lead.

quinine: A liquid made from tree bark used as a medicine in colonial America.

samp: Porridge made from boiled corn.

settle: A long bench with a solid back.

snake ball: In colonial America, a useless home remedy consisting of snake parts mixed with chalk.

stocks: A wooden apparatus in which a person who was being punished sat with the legs outstretched and immovable.

tanner: A leather maker.

tattling stick: A stick with leather straps attached to the end, used to punish children.

thatch: Bundles of dried straw and reeds used in building early colonial houses.

trencher: A bowl-like dish from which two diners ate.

wainwright: A person who made wagons and carts.

warming pan: A small metal container filled with embers, used to warm sheets on cold nights.

wattle: Interwoven tree branches used in building early colonial houses.

Time Line

1607
English settlers establish the Jamestown Colony in what is now Virginia.

1625
Dutch settlers establish the town of New Amsterdam (later New York City) on Manhattan Island.

1635
Massachusetts settlers pass a law banning the building of farmhouses more than half a mile from the central meetinghouse.

1636
Harvard College is established in what is now Cambridge, Massachusetts.

1640
Japanese leaders ban all foreigners from Japan.

1644
The Puritans prohibit Christmas celebrations and customs.

1647
The Massachusetts Bay Colony requires that all children must attend school.

1648
Shah Jahan, emperor of India, erects the magnificent Taj Mahal in India as a monument to his deceased wife.

1676
Virginia's Nathaniel Bacon leads a bloody rebellion against that colony's government.

1713
A terrible measles epidemic strikes residents in Massachusetts.

1716
Dancing classes are first taught at Virginia's College of William and Mary.

1721
A Boston doctor first attempts to inoculate patients against smallpox.

1741
George Frideric Handel composes the famous choral work *The Messiah*.

1745
Benjamin Rush, the first great medical researcher in the English colonies, is born.

1746
The College of New Jersey, later Princeton University, is established.

1752
Noted inventor Benjamin Franklin experiments with electricity.

1762
Catherine II (the Great) becomes ruler of Russia.

1776
Britain's thirteen North American colonies declare their independence and the American Revolution begins.

For More Information

Books

James Deetz and Patricia S. Deetz, *The Times of Their Lives: Life, Love, and Death in Plymouth Colony*. New York: Anchor, 2001. Deetz and Deetz are first-rate scholars who present a fresh, compelling, and well-documented look at the real history of Plymouth Colony in this book.

Sydney G. Fisher, *Men, Women, and Manners in Colonial America*. Whitefish, MT: Kessinger, 2007. This book discusses colonial manners and customs.

Elizabeth Gemming, *Huckleberry Hill: Child Life in Old Colonial New England*. New York: Crowell, 1968. This book is a well-written study of children's lives and activities in the colonial era.

David F. Hawke, *Everyday Life in Early America*. New York: Harper and Row, 1989. This book is a well-written exploration of early colonial life, including farms, houses, health, race relations, and manners and morals.

James Marten, ed., *Children in Colonial America*. New York: New York University Press, 2007. This is an excellent collection of essays by leading scholars.

John C. Miller, *The First Frontier: Life in Colonial America*. Lanham, MD: University Press of America, 1986. This book offers a very thoughtful and useful look at life and customs in colonial America, featuring numerous colorful primary source quotations.

Elizabeth G. Speare, *Life in Colonial America*. New York: Random House, 1963. Although somewhat dated now, Speare's very well-researched and well-written book on colonial America remains useful.

Alan Taylor, *American Colonies: The Settling of North America*. New York: Penguin, 2001. This is an extremely well-researched and nearly definitive treatment of the colonies by Alan Taylor, a Pulitzer Prize–winning scholar.

Edwin Tunis, *Colonial Craftsmen and the Beginnings of American Industry*. Baltimore: Johns Hopkins University Press, 1999. This is a thorough, nicely illustrated volume that covers every major colonial craft.

———, *Colonial Living*. Baltimore, MD: Johns Hopkins University Press, 1999. Another fine book by Edwin Tunis, this one covers many areas of colonial life, including furniture, food, weaving, clothing, tools, ships, travel, and much more.

James M. Volo and Dorothy D. Volo, *Daily Life on the Old Colonial Frontier*. Westport, CT: Greenwood, 2002.

This book offers an extremely well-researched and informative look at daily life in the rural areas of colonial America.

Louis B. Wright, *The Cultural Life of the American Colonies, 1607–1763*. New York: Harper and Row, 2002. This classic volume examines education, learning, libraries, drama, music, the decorative arts, and more in the colonial era. Highly recommended.

———, *Everyday Life in Colonial America*. New York: Putnam's, 1965. Although older now, this study of the subject by Louis B. Wright, a leading scholar in the field, remains one of the best.

Web Sites

Colonial Diseases and Cures (http://homepages.rootsweb.ancestry.com/~sam/disease.html). Provides useful information about common illnesses in colonial America.

Colonial House: Interactive History (http://www.pbs.org/wnet/colonialhouse/history/index.html). Allows the user to see and hear reconstructions of various aspects of life in the American colonies.

Colonial Occupations (http://homepages.rootsweb.ancestry.com/~sam/occupation.html). Contains a long, authoritative list of colonial jobs.

Colonial Williamsburg, Official Site (http://www.history.org/almanack/life/life.cfm). The official site for one of the country's premiere reconstructions of colonial American life.

Education in the 13 American Colonies (http://www.socialstudiesforkids.com/articles/ushistory/13coloniesschool.htm). A kid-friendly general introduction to the subject.

Farming in the 13 American Colonies (http://www.socialstudiesforkids.com/articles/ushistory/13coloniesfarm.htm). Tells the basics about farmers and their crops in colonial times.

Women's Role Before and During the Colonial Period (http://www.webconnections.com/MES5th/ColonialWomen_B4.htm). A very informative look at colonial women, with numerous photos of modern women in authentic colonial costumes.

Index

Picture Credits

Cover photos: © North Wind/North
  Wind Picture Archives; Image
  copyright Diego Cervo, 2009. Used
  under license from Shutterstock.com.
Buyenlarge/Hulton Archive/Getty
  Images, 68
General Photographic Agency/Hulton
  Archive/Getty Images, 65
Hulton Archive/Getty Images, 47, 50
Image copyright © The Metropolitan
  Museum of Art/Art Resource, NY, 17

MPI/Hulton Archive/Getty Images, 39,
  53, 70
© North Wind/North Wind Picture
  Archives, 8, 9, 15, 19, 21, 24, 25, 29,
  33, 36, 38, 42, 44, 54, 57, 59, 63, 74,
  77, 79
North Wind/Nancy Carter/North
  Wind Picture Archives, 45
Dick Smith/Hulton Archive/Getty
  Images, 13

About the Author

Historian and award-winning author Don Nardo has written many books for young adults about American history, among them *The Salem Witch Trials*, *The Sons of Liberty*, *The Declaration of Independence*, *The Mexican-American War*, and *The Great Depression*. He has also written biographies of presidents Thomas Jefferson, Andrew Johnson, and Franklin D. Roosevelt; several volumes about Native American history and culture; and a survey of the weapons and tactics used in the American Revolution. Nardo lives with his wife, Christine, in Massachusetts.